Sports Law in Finland

Sports Law in Finland

Antti Aine

This book was originally published as a monograph in the International Encyclopaedia of Laws/Sports Law.

Founding Editor: Roger Blanpain
General Editor: Frank Hendrickx
Volume Editor: Michele Colucci

Wolters Kluwer

Published by:
Kluwer Law International B.V.
PO Box 316
2400 AH Alphen aan den Rijn
The Netherlands
E-mail: lrs-sales@wolterskluwer.com
Website: www.wolterskluwer.com/en/solutions/kluwerlawinternational

Sold and distributed by:
Wolters Kluwer Legal & Regulatory U.S.
920 Links Avenue
Landisville, PA 17538
United States of America
E-mail: customer.service@wolterskluwer.com

ISBN 978-94-035-4037-5

e-Book: ISBN 978-94-035-4047-4
web-PDF: ISBN 978-94-035-4057-3

The Author

Dr Antti Aine is Professor of Sports Law at the University of Helsinki, Faculty of Law and at the University of Turku, Faculty of Law. Dr Aine has written extensively on sports law, EU and Finnish competition law, contract law and tort law. He has led various research projects. Dr Aine is Expert Member of the Market Court, Finland.

The Author

Table of Contents

List of Abbreviations

AKK-Motorsport	*AKK-Motorsport ry*, Finnish Automobile Sport Federation
CAS	Court of Arbitration for Sport
CHL	Champions Hockey League
EBU	European Broadcasting Union
ECJ	European Court of Justice
EGC	General Court of European Union
FHPA	*Suomen Jääkiekkoilijat ry*, Finnish Ice Hockey Players' Association
FIA	Fédération Internationale de l'Automobile
FIFA	Federation Internationale de Football Association
FINADA	*Suomen Antidopingtoimikunta ADT ry*, Finnish Anti-doping Agency
FINCIS	Finnish Center for Integrity in Sports
FIS	*Fédération Internationale de Ski*, International Ski Federation
FIVB	*Fédération Internationale de Volleyball*, International Volleyball Federation
FOA	*Suomen Olympia-Akatemia*, Finnish Olympic Academy
FOC	*Suomen Olympiakomitea ry*, Finnish Olympic Committee
FSC	Finnish Sports Confederation
FSFs	Finnish Sports Federations
HPU	*Huippu-urheilu yksikkö, Suomen Olympiakomitea ry*, High Performance Unit
IAAF	International Association of Athletics Federations
IIHF	International Ice Hockey Federation
IOA	International Olympic Academy
IOC	International Olympic Committee
ISU	International Skating Union
KHO	*Korkein hallinto-oikeus*, Supreme Administrative Court, Finland

List of Abbreviations

KKO	*Korkein oikeus*, Supreme Court, Finland
SJL	*Suomen Jääkiekkoliitto ry*, Finnish Ice Hockey Association
SML	*Suomen Moottoriliitto ry*, Finnish Motor Association
SM League	*Jääkiekon SM-liiga Oy*, Finnish Hockey League Ltd
SUL	*Suomen Urheiluliitto ry*, Finnish Athletics Federation
TFEU	Treaty on the Functioning of the European Union
TUEC	Therapeutic Use Exemption Committee
UEFA	Union of European Football Associations
WADA	World Anti-doping Agency

General Introduction

Chapter 1. Introduction

§1. General

1. Finland is one of the leading countries in Europe for physical activity. According to the National Sports Survey, 92% of women and 87% of men engage in physical activity and sports at least twice a week.[1] Non-governmental organizations have a central role in the Finnish sports system. Sports activities are organized mainly by sports clubs and federations. The number of these organizations is relatively high in Finland: there are around 7,800 sports clubs, 130 sports federations, and other national sports organizations in Finland. Over 20% of the population (EUR 1.1 million) are members of sports clubs. Most (97%) of the clubs are non-profit making which means that they are founded for the common realization of a non-profit purpose. In practice, most of the funding for sports clubs comes from members and parents.

2. Voluntary activities form the basis of the Finnish sports culture. There are approximately 600,000 volunteers and leaders in sports clubs and federations.[2] In Finland, 10% of the population takes part in voluntary sport work in their leisure time, and the value of this work is estimated to be EUR 1.5 billion per year. According to the National Sports Survey, 43% of Finnish children and youth are active in sports clubs.[3] The most popular sport is cycling. The most popular sports for boys are football and floorball, whereas for girls, jogging and swimming are the most popular sports.

3. Statistics indicate that 92% of boys and 91% of girls are involved in sports and physical activities.[4] More women than men are sufficiently physically active in terms of health, although differences between the genders are small. Fifty-eight per cent of sport club members are male and 42% are female. Of the 600,000 volunteers involved, 43% are women. Women account for 32% of the board members of

1. *National Sports Survey 2009–2010 (Adults)*, 6 (SLU:n julkaisusarja 7/2010).
2. *Annual Report 2010*, 17 (Ministry of Education and Culture).
3. *National Sports Survey 2009–2010 (Children and Young People)*, 13 (SLU:n julkaisusarja 7/2010).
4. *National Sports Survey 2009–2010 (Children and Young People)*, 6 (SLU:n julkaisusarja 7/2010).

sports organizations, 16% of the presidents of sports organizations, and 34% of the executive directors of sports organizations.[5]

4. Public administration also plays an important role in promoting sport.[6] According to the Sports Act (390/2015), the Government and the municipalities are responsible for creating general preconditions for sport. The Ministry of Education and Culture is responsible for the overall management, development, and coordination of matters pertaining to the national sports policy, and is assisted in sports matters by the National Sports Council. At the regional level, responsibility for creating opportunities and facilities for engagement in physical activities rests with provincial sports departments and at the local level with the municipalities. In practice, responsibilities relating to sports promotion are directed at the central and local sports administrations and, as regards actual sports provision, at sports organizations and clubs.

5. Competitive and top-level sports are an important part of Finnish sports culture.[7] The Government has a duty to create favourable conditions for competitive and performance sports. There are many reasons for the national significance of top-level sports. Relevance of top-level sports derives from its entertainment value and the experiences of communality and identification sport offers spectators. Additionally, top-level sports are important in terms of the national economy. However, competitive sports largely depend on volunteer work: less than 3% of the sports clubs (about 200) have professional athletes. There are about 1,100 professional athletes in Finland, that is, athletes who earn their principal income from sports and about 1,200 coaches who earn at least half of their income from coaching.

§2. Vision and Strategy

6. Physical activity has many functions in modern societies. It is a significant factor for the well-being of the population at all stages of life, and also supports the growth and development of children and young people.[8] It can also help maintain work and functional capacity, increase older citizens' independence and joy for life, as well as add to a sense of social solidarity. Moreover, an increase in physical activity can create considerable savings in public finances.

7. There are many challenges for the national sports policy in Finland, and although the above-mentioned positive benefits of physical activity and sport are widely recognized, the overall physical activity of the population has decreased and

5. *Sport and Equality 2017. Current State and Changes of Gender Equality in Finland*, 58–59 (Publications of the Ministry of Education and Culture 2018:6).
6. *Government Resolution on Policies Promoting Sport and Physical Activity*, 9–10 (Ministry of Education Publication 2009:44).
7. *Government Resolution on Policies Promoting Sport and Physical Activity*, 12 (Ministry of Education Publication 2009:44).
8. *Government Resolution on Policies Promoting Sport and Physical Activity*, 9, 17–18 (Ministry of Education Publication 2009:44).

individual differences in physical activity have increased.[9] The varied opportunities for sport have only partly been used. The dramatic changes in society have posed a challenge to the Government and non-governmental organizations when evaluating the current activities in sports and physical culture, but they have also provided new opportunities. Ageing, regional variations, technological development, climate change, sedentary lifestyles, lifestyle-related diseases, and many other recognizable factors can be seen as catalysts for change.

8. The overall aim of Finnish sports and physical activity has been crystallized in the words of Vision 2020: 'We are the world's most physically active nation – 2020'.[10] Sports and physical activity are seen as a way of life for people of all ages. Some crucial ideas can be presented in order to achieve these aims. It is essential to increase the quantity and quality of physical activity in the whole population throughout life. At the same time, the motives and experiences that encourage people to participate in sports and physical activity are of the utmost importance. The general aim is that everyone will have the possibility to practice sports and physical activity according to their own abilities and goals.

9. Vision 2020 sees sports and physical activity as a way of life. They are an integral part of childhood and youth and the most significant factors contributing to well-being. Many different types of organizations, institutions, and communities are needed in order to reach this goal; sports clubs, schools, families, local authorities, companies, and many others can encourage and enable people to engage in sport and exercise.

10. According to Vision 2020, there are many factors that encourage us all to exercise at different points in our lives: experiences such as physical fitness, competing, and participating in social activities can lead to an enjoyment of physical activity and sports. Finnish sports organizations support these experiences in order to promote a physically active lifestyle, but in addition, sports and physical activity require enabling and activating conditions which means the appropriate facilities.

11. Various aspects of sport and physical activity have been evaluated in Vision 2020. It recognizes that sports and physical activity have intrinsic values, for example, joy, health, and a meaningful lifestyle.[11] At the same time, sport and physical activity are of instrumental value to society: among other things, they significantly enhance social well-being, increase public health, and prevent social marginalization.

9. *Government Resolution on Policies Promoting Sport and Physical Activity*, 9 (Ministry of Education Publication 2009:44).
10. *The Finnish Sports Confederation, Strategy 2020.*
11. *See also Sport and Equality. Current State and Changes of Gender Equality in Finland*, 30–31 (Publications of the Ministry of Education and Culture 2012:13, Helsinki 2012).

Chapter 2. Development of Sports Law in Finland

§1. General Background

12. Sport encompasses many dimensions and concepts, and it is important to recognize these in order to define the relevant contexts where sports law may be applied. Competitive sport constitutes a central context in sports law; its typical features include competing, rules and results which can be measured and evaluated.[12]

13. It is possible to distinguish between professional sport and competitive sport. There is an economic dimension of commercialization in professional sport. Athletes, clubs and other related undertakings have commercial goals to achieve in professional sport. The media have an important role in commercializing sports events. Sport is actually a part of the entertainment market and is in competition with other entertainment services. In practice, clubs can be seen as providers of entertainment services.

14. Individuals have different reasons for participating in sporting activities. Fitness sports are based on individuals' desire to improve their physical capacity and health. However, it is important to notice that there are also commercial aspects to fitness sport. Business undertakings provide services which can be used by individuals when they participate in sporting activities. Health Sport can also be mentioned as another concept in sport; it refers to all the physical exercise individuals take to improve their physical condition.

15. Different concepts of sport and parallel contexts of sport based on these concepts can make it difficult to develop the doctrine of sports law. There are limited possibilities for finding a basis of common values for sports law. At the same time, social and educational goals must be taken into consideration when applying sports law, since the doctrine of sports law does not only include dimensions dealing with competitions and championships.

16. The development of sports law can be seen as an important example of the juridification of sports. Nowadays, legal regulation and discretion affect sport more than ever. This development has caused many difficult situations in the Finnish sports system, one example being the match-fixing scandal in Finnish baseball in 1998. The concept of juridification is very wide and partly open, and it is an essential task of sports law to define what this concept actually means in sport.

17. The borderline between legal and sport-related questions is important in sports law. It is possible for an individual case to be decided by a court of law rather than a sports organization. This is a question that relates to the jurisdiction of courts

12. Johan Steenbergen & Jan Tamboer, *Ethics and the Double Character of Sport*, in *Ethics and Sport*, 37 (M.J McNamee & S.J. Parry eds, Routledge 1998), https://www.taylorfrancis.com/books/edit/10.4324/9780203476642/ethics-sport-mcnamee-parry.

in Finland. Traditionally, a negative position has been taken in Finnish legal literature in regard to this question.[13] According to this view, courts of law have no jurisdiction to decide cases related to sports competitions. On the contrary, it is possible to argue that such jurisdiction may be justified in order to guarantee systematic application of competition rules.

18. The Supreme Court has defined the preconditions for bringing decisions made by sports organizations before a court of law.[14] The case in question involved doping where an ineligibility sanction was imposed on an athlete who had violated an anti-doping rule. The Supreme Court emphasized the overall effects of the ineligibility sanction on the athlete's legal position and fundamental rights. In particular, the athlete's opportunities to use his right to engage in commercial activity conferred in section 18 of the Constitution of Finland were seen as decisive. The Supreme Court decided to hear the case for consideration but did not change the period of the athlete's ineligibility.

19. The juridification of sport can be regarded as a harmful phenomenon because it reduces sports organizations' freedom to operate. It is possible to argue that limiting this freedom is harmful because something valuable in sport is lost as a result of this development. Yet the main principle should be the implementation of sports organizations' own rules as far as possible in sport. Therefore, implementation of legal rules should be as limited as possible.

20. This perspective is interesting and represents a traditional way of thinking in sport. It is closely linked to the freedom of association of sports organizations which is protected in section 13 of the Constitution of Finland. It gives an association the right to decide its rules and activities, as well as who can become a member. Freedom of association is based on ideas of an individual's freedom and the right to form an association, but it also protects associations as legal persons and guarantees their freedom of action.[15]

21. Freedom of association has an important function in protecting the independence of sports organizations of public authorities. However, the freedom of association protected in section 13 of the Constitution is not absolute: an individual's right to freedom of association has to be weighed against other fundamental rights and the interests of society. Most of the fundamental rights are relational in nature and this limits the freedom of action of sports organizations.

22. In practice, there is an interplay between legal rules and the rules adopted by sports organizations in legal discretion. There are numerous examples of this: a contract of employment between a player and a club, disciplinary decisions before courts of law, applying European Union (EU) free movement provisions and EU

13. Tauno Ellilä, *Oikeudenkäynti ja täytäntöönpano*, 106–114 (2nd ed., Helsinki WSOY 1965).
14. KKO 1998:122.
15. Heikki Halila, *Toimivaltajako yhdistyksissä*, 241–245 (Helsinki Suomalainen Lakimiesyhdistys 1993).

competition law to sport and basic rights and human rights in sport. The main consideration here concerns a sustainable balance between both regimes. It is not a one-way phenomenon, rather the special features of the sports context have to be taken into consideration when applying legal norms. In this connection, the smooth functioning of sports competitions and the pyramid structure of European sports are of relevance.

23. Different legislative strategies are chosen in the governance of sport and related issues. In this respect, a basic distinction can be made between interventionist and non-interventionist legal systems. Finland belongs to the group of non-interventionist legal systems. The public governance of sports in Finland is based on the Sports Act (390/2015). According to section 1 of the Act, its purpose is to promote recreational, competitive and top-level sports and associated civic activity, to promote the population's well-being and health and to support children's and young people's growth and development through sports.

24. Neither athletes' rights and duties nor the relationships between athletes and sports organizations are defined in the Sports Act. Practical decisions have to be made by sports and athletes' organizations. The crucial starting point is freedom of association, but there are specific regulations relating to sport and the legal position of athletes in legislation, for example, the Athletes' Accident and Pension Security Act (276/2009). In addition, there are other sport-specific regulations in certain acts, for example, in tax legislation.

25. Generally, it is possible to say that public governance has increased in sports during the last decades. This governance can have different forms; it can be indirect in nature. This is often a very effective way of governing sports. Indirect governance is based on state subsidies for national and regional sports organizations. The conditions for these subsidies can be set by the Ministry of Education and Culture, and may concern, for example, sports organizations' commitment to the ethical values of sport, which may include equality, tolerance and fair play in sports.

26. Occasionally, there have been discussions in Finland about increasing public governance in sport. This matter was of relevance when a working group prepared a legislative proposal on disciplinary procedures and sanctions in professional sport.[16] Although this proposal did not lead to any legislation, disciplinary processes and sanctions can have an important effect on an athlete's legal position and fundamental rights especially in professional sport. Restrictions on the freedom to engage in commercial activity should be based on legislation. Additionally, it would be possible to consider laying down specific provisions on employment relations in team sports.

27. Decisions made at the EU level have accelerated the process of the juridification of sports. The Lisbon Treaty, which came into force on 1 December 2009, includes for the first time in an EU Treaty an explicit provision on sport. According

16. *SLU:n työsuhdetyöryhmän mietintö 5.10.1999* (The Finnish Sports Federation Helsinki 1999).

to Article 165 Treaty on the Functioning of the European Union (TFEU), the Union must contribute to the development of quality education by encouraging cooperation between Member States and, if necessary, by supporting and supplementing their action, while fully respecting the responsibility of the Member States for the content of teaching and the organization of education systems and their cultural and linguistic diversity. The Union must contribute to the promotion of European sporting issues while taking into account the specific nature of sport, its structures based on voluntary activity and its social and educational function.

28. It is essential to notice that the above-mentioned Article concerns not only sport as an economic activity but also amateur and recreational sports. However, it provides only a weak legal basis for EU action. In order to contribute to the achievement of the objectives referred to in Article 165 TFEU, the European Parliament and the Council, acting in accordance with the ordinary legislative procedure, after consulting the Economic and Social Committee and the Committee of the Regions, may adopt incentive measures, excluding any harmonization of the laws and regulations of the Member States, and the Council, on a proposal from the Commission, may adopt recommendations.

29. In practice, Article 165 TFEU can provide an important legal basis in cases where the EU wants to finance different projects concerning sports. Furthermore, the Article can also be of relevance when solving cross-border problems in sport such as match-fixing. However, the Article does not appear to have had a crucial effect on the application of EU free movement and competition law provisions. It is possible to assume that governance based on EU legislation will increase in sport in the near future. There are various problems in sports, such as doping and spectator violence, which may be possible to solve using EU legislation. However, the legal basis for this may not necessarily be Article 165 TFEU, and a different legal basis may be used on these occasions. In this regard, an interesting further dimension concerns the competence of the EU to regulate national criminal law sanctions.

30. Sports organizations can adopt different strategies concerning the juridification of sports. It may be argued that it is not a very wise decision to remain passive and just wait for the decisions of courts and other tribunals. Rather, sports organizations should be pro-active and develop their own internal norms and procedures. Juridification increases the material requirements for internal norms and procedures in sports. This development can take different forms. An important example is the internal dispute solution mechanism in sport, such as the Finnish Sports Arbitration Board and the Court of Arbitration for Sport (CAS). It is possible to predict that polycentrism will increase among the legal ways of governing sport.

31. Alternatively, it is always important to know the context when applying legal norms in sport. The context of sport has played a crucial role in criminal law cases concerning violence in ice hockey matches in Finland.[17] The Supreme Court took into consideration the special features of ice hockey when it applied criminal law

17. KKO 1996:74 and KKO 1997:129.

norms in these cases. The rules of a game, established custom and the spirit of a game are often relevant factors that have to be taken into account in legal discretion, but this does not undermine the normative content of legal discretion. Similarly, modern Western societies have approved of giving sports organizations the competence to regulate sports. The World Anti-Doping Agency (WADA) represents a prime example of this development. The Agency is a non-governmental organization which is responsible for the World Anti-Doping Code regulating anti-doping violations, procedures and sanctions; the Code has a large effect on the legal position of athletes.

32. The juridification of sport has also affected the legal position of associations, such as sports federations and clubs. Associations have a legally guaranteed freedom to make decisions concerning their members and activities. These decisions can only be challenged on the specific juridical grounds mentioned in the Finnish Associations Act. However, it should be noted that resolutions adopted by associations often have significant effects on the fundamental rights and legal position of athletes. In practice, these decisions can concern, for example, the nomination of athletes for international championships and other competitions. In Finland, the Finnish Sports Arbitration Board can, under certain conditions, decide such matters.

33. The juridification of sport is partly based on the relevance of fundamental rights and human rights, both of which have been strengthened in Finland during the past decades. It is important to note that fundamental rights can also have horizontal effects between individuals, and this dimension increases the possibilities of applying fundamental rights in the context of sport.[18] There are many questions in sport, such as disciplinary procedures in professional sport and the lifetime ineligibility sanction in anti-doping cases, which can be answered systematically on the basis of fundamental rights. A comprehensive method is needed when applying legal discretion. Furthermore, research in sports law can play an important role in assisting the development of the systematic features of this discretion.

§2. Academic Research

I. Background

34. In Finland, the juridification of sport began in the early 1990s and is a central factor in the development of sports law. It is possible to say that the process of juridification came as a surprise to Finnish sports organizations.[19] There are many national and international cases which can be seen as providing an impetus for the process of juridification in sport. In the case of Joensuun Kataja Basketball Club,

18. *See*, e.g., Heikki Halila, *Oikeudellistuva urheilu*, 384–386 (Helsinki Talentum 2006), and Heikki Halila & Olli Norros, *Urheiluoikeus*, 153–174 (Helsinki Alma Talent 2017).
19. Heikki Halila, *Oikeudellistuva urheilu*, 21–24 (Helsinki Talentum 2006).

the Finnish Competition and Consumer Authority was asked to rule on whether conditions set by the Finnish Basketball Association for participation in the National Basketball League were acceptable in the context of competition law.[20] At the EU level, the *Bosman* case radically changed the structures of European Football and had an important effect on Finnish football clubs and players.[21] This development led to legal questions gaining a central position in sport.

35. A typical feature of sports law in Finland is that it has developed by critically evaluating traditional practices in sport and systematizing the relevant case law. The starting point of this process has been practical: the aim of research in sports law has been to give sports federations, sports clubs and athletes solutions to problems following the juridification of sport. Creating best practices for sport has been the central task of sports law in Finland.

36. Quasi-legal instruments which do not have legally binding force (soft law) have played an important role in the development of sports law in Finland since the 1990s. Self-regulation is still a crucial legal instrument used by Finnish Sports Federations (FSFs), and model rules for sports clubs are an example of relevant self-regulation. It seems that the amount and also the quality of self-regulation have increased at the same time as the juridification of sport has acquired new dimensions. The development of Finnish society and the juridification process have forced an improvement in the internal rules and practices in sport.

37. The juridification process has also affected institutional questions concerning sport in Finland. It has meant the emergence of a new way of evaluating the need for legislation on sport-related matters. The importance of legal dispute solution has increased during the last decades, and FSFs and clubs are required to decide legal questions more than ever when individuals are ready to refer to their fundamental and human rights. In this context, FSFs have many challenges to overcome.

II. Early Years of Finnish Sports Law

38. Themes related to sport have been discussed at an early stage in Finnish legal literature; an example is Paavo Kekomäki's dissertation which was published in 1933.[22] A central theme of the dissertation was whether an athlete can be regarded as a professional criminal; Kekomäki answered the question in the affirmative. The basic formulation of the dissertation's research questions is very much related to the time at which it was written and the fundamental division between professional and amateur sports.

20. The Competition Council 9.2.1998, 7/359/96, and the Supreme Administrative Court 2000:2.
21. Case C-415/93 *ASBL v. Bosman, Royal club de liégeois SA v. Bosman and others, UEFA v. Bosman*, (1995) ECR I 4921.
22. Paavo Kekomäki, *Ammattimaisten ja tavanomaisten rikosten käsitteistä* (Helsinki 1933).

39. Inkeri Anttila's dissertation, published in 1946, has as its central theme the relevance of consent given by a victim in criminal law.[23] This theme has close connections to violence in sport since criminal law doctrine can be applied in sport. At the same time, sports rules are of relevance when applying norms of criminal law. Valid consent can be given for acts which are against the rules of the game but, at the same time, are typical of the game. This discretion enhances the interplay between legal norms and self-regulation in sport which is still a relevant issue in sport.

40. Themes related to sports law have also been discussed in the law of obligations and in procedural law in Finland. In his book on the law of obligations in 1965, Yrjö Hakulinen discussed how voluntary consent to participate in a sporting competition can affect an athlete's right to receive compensation for injuries sustained during that sporting competition.[24] This question is still relevant in sports law. Tauno Ellilä has examined the jurisdiction of courts of law over decisions made by sports officials.[25] Typically, this question concerns situations where an athlete has won a race or a championship by violating the rules and regulations of a sport. Ellilä came to the conclusion that decisions made by sports officials are internal matters within sports and they cannot be challenged before a court of law.

41. Early discussions concerning sport and its governance in Finnish legal literature do not prove that the doctrine of sports law had started to develop. On the contrary, issues related to sport were discussed as part of the general legal system and in the context of traditional branches of law. Nevertheless, these early discussions emphasized the juridical importance of sport-related questions and the obvious need to resolve the problems raised.

III. Recent Developments in Finnish Sports Law

42. The development of sports law in Finland can be described as a process which has different layers. Esko Linnakangas' dissertation, published in 1984, can be regarded as one of the starting points of recent Finnish sports law.[26] Linnakangas concentrated on investigating how the central values and aims of tax legislation can be applied in sport-related cases, and viewed sport mainly in the context of cultural policy and its requirements.

43. Linnakangas' main task was to solve legal problems concerning tax law, thus there is no detailed discussion of the doctrine of sports law in his dissertation. However, the dissertation provides an interesting survey of the history and financing of sport, as well as the history of taxation. It is also essential, in Linnakangas' opinion,

---

23. Inkeri Anttila, *Loukatun suostumus oikeudenvastaisuuden poistavana tekijänä* (Helsinki Suomalainen Lakimiesyhdistys 1946).
24. Y.J. Hakulinen, *Velvoiteoikeus I*, 278 (2nd ed., Helsinki Kirjayhtymä 1965).
25. Tauno Ellilä, *Oikeudenkäynti ja täytäntöönpano*, 106–114 (2nd ed., Helsinki WSOY 1965).
26. Esko Linnakangas, *Urheilu ja verotus* (Helsinki Lakimiesliiton Kustannus 1984).

that the peculiar context of sport was taken into consideration when applying tax law, and this has continued to be a typical feature of sports law in Finland. After his dissertation, Linnakangas has continued to explore the relationships between tax law and sport in his literary production.

44. Heikki Halila is regarded as the founding father of sports law in Finland. His research activities have their origins in civil law and the law of associations, and typically focus on legal problems concerning sport in these legal contexts. Halila's book *Oikeudellistuva urheilu*, published in 2006, can be seen as his master work in the field of sports law.[27] Many interesting and important themes concerning the juridification of sport and sports law are discussed in this book. A general work on sports law by Halila and Olli Norros was published in 2017.[28] Halila has also published numerous articles on sports law,[29] some of which have appeared in Nordic journals and books.[30]

45. Lauri Tarasti is a distinguished expert on sports law, the law of associations and legal dispute resolution in sport. He has focused in particular on legal questions related to doping, and has discussed legal procedures and dispute settlement mechanisms in international sports federations. His main work in sports law concentrates on legal dispute procedures in international doping cases.[31] One of his main ideas is that disciplinary procedures in doping cases cannot be considered as being equivalent to criminal procedures.

46. Sports law has close connections to the law of associations in Finland, and the work of Risto Riitesuo exemplifies this connection. He has examined decision-making procedures in associations,[32] a theme that is highly relevant to sports federations and sports clubs. Riitesuo has also discussed questions related to the legal basis of disciplinary procedures,[33] concentrating, for example, the binding effect of disciplinary decisions on athletes and other persons, the kinds of sanctions that can be imposed in disciplinary procedures and the organization of the decision-making procedure in associations.

---

27. Heikki Halila, *Oikeudellistuva urheilu* (Helsinki Talentum 2006).
28. Heikki Halila & Olli Norros, *Urheiluoikeus* (Helsinki Alma Talent 2017).
29. Heikki Halila, *Urheilusopimukset*, 278–302 (in Heikki Halila & Mika Hemmo (eds), Sopimustyypit (2nd ed., Helsinki Talentum 2008)), Heikki Halila, *Miten tehokkaasti urheilun oikeusturvalautakunnassa saadaan oikeusturvaa?*, Defensor Legis, 9–33 (1998), Heikki Halila, *Urheilun oikeusturvalautakunnan tila ja tulevaisuus*, Urheilu ja oikeus, 5–14 (2002), Heikki Halila, *Idrottsrätten som specifikt rättsområde*, Tidskrift utgiven av Juridiska Föreningen i Finland, 725–729 (2002).
30. Heikki Halila, *Vad är känneteckande för idrottsjuridiken*, 7–18 (in Heikki Halila & Olli Rauste (eds), Finskt-svenskt idrottsjuridiskt symposium i Helsingfors 1999 (Helsingfors Urheiluoikeuden yhdistys 1999)), Heikki Halila, *Disciplinära åtgärder mot professionella idrottare*, 37–42, in Svenskt idrottsjuridik föreningen, Artikelsamling, Idrottsjuridisk skriftserie Nr. 5 (2000).
31. Lauri Tarasti, *Legal Solutions in International Doping Cases* (SEP Milan 2000).
32. Risto Riitesuo, *Yhdistyksen kokousmenettely* (Helsinki Lakimiesliiton kustannus 2004).
33. Risto Riitesuo, *Erottaminen ja kurinpitomenettely yhdistyksessä* (Helsinki Lakimiesliiton kustannus 2001).

47. Some of the Finnish legal research in the field of sports law has been published internationally. A good example is Mikko Huttunen's dissertation which was approved by the European University Institute, Florence, on 25 February 2000.[34] This dissertation lies at the intersection of labour law and EU Law (free movement of workers) and takes up the question of the legal position of professional sportsmen under Finnish, English and EU law. Unfortunately, since the publication of this dissertation, legal discussions on this theme have been rather rare in Finland.

48. Several important books and publications on sports law appeared in Finland in the 1990s; a leading example is a general work on sports law by Olli Rauste published in 1997.[35] The book covers a wide range of topics, many of which have been essential for the development of sports law in Finland. Rauste takes into consideration legal discussions of sports law in the United States (US), but the perspective of the book is mainly limited to economic and commercial aspects of sport, and this can be seen as its weakness. Despite this criticism, the book was, and still is, a brave attempt to enlarge the area covered by sports law in Finland. Additionally, Rauste published a book on legal rules governing children's and youths' sports activities in 2017 and a book on ethical issues in sports in 2023.[36]

49. Since 2010, at least three very interesting monographs concerning sports law have been published in Finland. In the first, Olli Norros investigates questions related to the organization of sports leagues.[37] Although legal dogmatics forms the initial starting point for his research, Norros applies a problem-based method which provides different perspectives for analysing sports leagues and their organization.

50. Norros' central research questions are clearly formulated: he intends to produce new information about legal norms as they relate to and are applied to sports organizations.[38] At the same time, Norros presents some other interesting research questions: he examines the different legal ways of organizing sports leagues. He states that it is essential to consider what kind of legal advantages and drawbacks are related to these options. This way of posing questions has close connections to legal dogmatics but, at the same time, the factual consequences have to be taken into consideration when evaluating these questions.

51. Norros has based his research on certain ideas about legal norms and their application.[39] Law and customs constitute strongly binding legal norms, and it is not legally possible to circumvent these norms based on reasons related to sport. Therefore, strongly binding sources of law are at the centre of Norros' argumentation.

34. Mikko Huttunen, *A Comparative Analysis of the Legal Position of Professional Sportsmen under Finnish, English and European Community Law. The Borderlines of Employment* (Florence European University Institute 2000).
35. Olli Rauste, *Urheiluoikeus* (Helsinki Lakimiesliiton Kustannus 1997).
36. Olli Rauste, *Lasten ja nuorten urheilun oikeussäännöt* (Helsinki Tietosanoma 2017), and Olli Rauste, *Kohti eettistä urheilua – Käytännön opas* (Helsinki Tietosanoma 2023).
37. Olli Norros, *Urheiluliigan organisointi* (Helsinki WSOYpro 2011).
38. Olli Norros, *Urheiluliigan organisointi*, 4–9 (Helsinki WSOYpro 2011).
39. *See* Aulis Aarnio, *The Rational as Reasonable*, 78–89 (Dordrecht Reidel 1987).

However, practical reasons or so-called real arguments can be taken into consideration when solving problems relating to the organization of sport leagues. He argues that it is essential to consider the legal status of these arguments in legal discretion and examine their relevance in relation to the other sources of law.

52. Norros aims to discover information about real-life practices in sports leagues.[40] According to Norros, relevant information can consist of internal rules and procedures in sports leagues and sports federations. In this regard, he concentrates on the Finnish national leagues in ice hockey, Finnish baseball, football, and floorball. In addition to written material, Norros carried out interviews in order to realize his research aims.

53. Norros utilizes both national and international research material. Although his research is concerned mainly with the Finnish legal system, he uses international research material as a point of comparison. He makes comparisons, for example, between the Finnish legal system and the US legal system. In addition, Norros applies a method which has close connections to corporate governance traditions. Here, he is interested in the basic principles of governance structures of sports leagues rather than all the practical details.

54. Essi Kinnunen's dissertation on doping crimes is the second important publication that has appeared in sports law in Finland since 2010.[41] Published in 2012, her research has a broad starting point: frequently, doping is regarded as a simple and straightforward phenomenon. Her wish to go beyond this self-evident façade has served as the inspiration for her research. Kinnunen points out how and why doping has become the object of criminal regulation, and the kinds of prerequisites the legal system sets forth for such regulation. The aim of the study is to examine how doping has been defined in domestic criminal law. In addition, the connection between criminal law and internal regulation within sport is evaluated.

55. Kinnunen's dissertation is based on an examination of the history of the juridification and regulation of doping crimes within the Finnish Criminal Code.[42] It analyses doping from various perspectives (e.g., the social status of sports, the development of the internal anti-doping regulation within sport, and the intersections of sports law and criminal law). Kinnunen uses a wide range of non-legal and legal material in her research. Thematically, it progresses from extensive juridification problematics to the detailed legal analysis of doping criminalization.

56. Kinnunen's study may be situated at the interface of sports law and criminal law.[43] It analyses the content of criminal regulation of doping employing the tools

40. Olli Norros, *Urheiluliigan organisointi*, 27–28 (Helsinki WSOYpro 2011).
41. Essi Kinnunen, *Dopingrikos urheilun ja rikosoikeuden leikkauspisteessä* (Helsinki Suomalainen Lakimiesyhdistys 2012).
42. Essi Kinnunen, *Dopingrikos urheilun ja rikosoikeuden leikkauspisteessä*, 84–90 (Helsinki Suomalainen Lakimiesyhdistys 2012).
43. Essi Kinnunen, *Dopingrikos urheilun ja rikosoikeuden leikkauspisteessä*, 93–97 (Helsinki Suomalainen Lakimiesyhdistys 2012).

of criminal law and criminal law theory. It also serves as a statement concerning the juridification of sports law and the position of sports law within the legal field. At the same time, it reviews the manner in which the juridification of sport manifests itself, as well as the background factors leading to the juridification of sport.

57. Kinnunen discusses the identity of sports law as a field of legal research by raising fundamental questions about the nature of the study of sports law, and about whether sports law research differs from other legal research about sport.[44] She presents the background and premises of sports law, and offers viewpoints about the manner in which sports law may be perceived within jurisprudence.

58. Kinnunen also examines the criminal regulation of doping and defines what kind of a phenomenon doping is from the point of view of criminal law by utilizing the theories and principles characteristic of criminal law.[45] She discusses the acceptability of doping criminalization, particularly against the backdrop formed by the criminalization principles of criminal law. In addition, she focuses on those aspects of the Finnish Criminal Code relating to doping crimes and examines the areas pertaining to the constituent elements that are problematic in terms of their interpretation.

59. Kinnunen is interested in fundamental questions of doping-related criminal policy in her dissertation.[46] She argues that it is essential to discuss how to control the use of doping substances. As with narcotics, these substances are associated with a fairly pronounced morally negative attitude, rendering it relatively easy to subject them to harsh criminal sanctions. The goal of anti-doping operations within the field of sport is to wage a war against doping which will result in its eradication. Kinnunen takes a critical stance towards the idea that this goal could also be the objective of a rational criminal and control policy pertaining to doping substances.

60. Esa Schön's dissertation on a team athlete's player contract was published in 2021.[47] Schön examines in his dissertation the contract models commonly used in team sports in Finland. The aim of the study is to define the special features of a professional athlete's player contract and to examine how the special features of a professional athlete's player contract affect its legal status as an employment contract. In addition, rights and duties of both contracting parties (i.e., the player and the club) are discussed in the study.

---

44. Essi Kinnunen, *Dopingrikos urheilun ja rikosoikeuden leikkauspisteessä*, 104–110 (Helsinki Suomalainen Lakimiesyhdistys 2012).
45. Essi Kinnunen, *Dopingrikos urheilun ja rikosoikeuden leikkauspisteessä*, 135–145 (Helsinki Suomalainen Lakimiesyhdistys 2012).
46. Essi Kinnunen, *Dopingrikos urheilun ja rikosoikeuden leikkauspisteessä*, 273–279 (Helsinki Suomalainen Lakimiesyhdistys 2012).
47. Esa Schön, *Pelaajasopimus. Tutkimus joukkueurheilijoiden pelaajasopimusten tyypillisestä sisällöstä, erityispiirteistä ja oikeusvaikutuksista* (Helsinki Unigrafia 2021).

61. There have been some studies concerning the relationship between competition law and sport.[48] This theme has also been relevant in practice. In some cases, the Finnish Competition and Consumer Authority has investigated the possibilities of sports federations controlling athlete's freedom to choose sponsors by contractual arrangements.[49] Furthermore, in a basketball case, the Authority has examined the relationship between competition law and those sport-related and economic conditions presented by the Finnish Basketball Association for participation in the National Basketball League.[50]

62. Various articles on sports law have been regularly published in Finnish law journals; published since 1999, *Urheilu ja oikeus* is the only journal that specializes in sports law in Finland. The Ministry of Culture and Education has financially supported the publication of articles and other academic works related to sports law, for example, it has established a publication series for Master of Laws theses concerning sports law. This has provided different lawyers and other readers with an opportunity to have new information about sports law and relevant case law. Furthermore, it is worth mentioning that the former FSF and the Finnish Sports Confederation (FSC) have published several reports on issues relevant to sports federations and athletes.

§3. Doctrine of Sports Law

63. The development of sports law can be seen as an important dimension of the juridification of sport. Some concrete examples can be mentioned here. Sports law has many important legal interfaces between sport and its self-governance. Various kinds of contracts are regularly negotiated and signed in sport; contracts can be used as legal instruments to bind organizations and athletes to engage in sport activities. Sports law has the task of evaluating the conditions under which contracts can be used to achieve this goal in sport.

64. The application of competition law in sport is another example of the kind of interface mentioned previously. The structure of sport is highly concentrated in Europe, and in practice, this structure can mean that sports organizations have a dominant market position in a relevant market.[51] Therefore, Article 102 TFEU can have an effect on sports organizations' possibilities to engage in business or other activities.

---

48. Antti Aine, *Competition Law and Sport*, 79–95 (in Heikki Halila (ed.), Nordiskt seminarium i idrottsjuridik 2006 (Vaajakoski Urheiluoikeuden yhdistys 2007)), Antti Aine, *Urheilu ja toimivat markkinat* (Helsinki Edita 2016), and Antti Aine, *The European Model of Sport and Competition Law*, Idrottsjuridisk skriftserie Nr 25, Artikelsamling 2020, Svensk Idrottsjuridisk Förening, 21–42.
49. The Finnish Competition and Consumer Authority 11.11.2004, 756/61/04, and the Market Court 215/06.
50. The Competition Council 9.2.1998, 7/359/96, and the Supreme Administrative Court 2000:2.
51. *See also* Lars Halgreen, *European Sports Law. A Comparative Analysis of the European and American Models of Sport* 64–65 (Kobenhavn Forlaget Thomson 2004).

65. Furthermore, an interesting interface exists between fundamental rights, human rights and sport. Fundamental rights and human rights are becoming increasingly important in Western democratic societies, and questions related to these rights are relevant in many situations in sport: one concrete example is the application of anti-doping rules.

66. In this context, one of the basic challenges of sport law is to find a workable method for research. In many cases, the method applied in sports law is legal dogmatics. Within this regime, it is possible to classify research methods in different ways, for example, norm-based methods and problem-based methods. Typically, a norm-based method leads to an evaluation of the conditions in which a certain norm has been applied and how this norm has generally been applied in case law. On the contrary, a problem-based method concentrates on an examination of the kinds of norms applicable to a concrete legal problem and on how to structure a comprehensive analysis based on these norms and relevant case law. Both methods are possible in sports law and both methods have been applied in sports law in Finland.[52] However, it seems that this distinction between different methods does not solve the crucial questions of sports law.

67. General doctrines form a solid basis for every branch of law, therefore, the fundamental question of sports law concerns the role of general doctrines in the future development of the discipline. In this way, sports law differs, for example, from sport and health sciences and social sciences although relevant research questions can, in some cases, be closely related to those of these disciplines.[53] Answers to this question are highly dependent on the way in which the position of sports law in the Finnish legal system is defined. Sports law can be understood only as a context where sports-related norms are applied. From this point of view, sports law has a limited scope of its own. Alternatively, it is possible to see that sports law has its own core values with the general doctrines forming a central idea.

68. There are many challenges when systematizing the general doctrines of sports law. It is possible to identify different aspects of legal discussions concerning the general doctrines of sports law. Therefore, it is difficult to describe an independent theory in sports law. At least in Finland, research activities in sports law have concentrated on practical issues. In addition, the fact that there are only some legal acts concerning sports-related matters might become an obstacle to the development of general doctrines. The legal basis for sports law in Finland is thin. It is too easy a choice to describe sports law as a collection of legal norms concerning sport.

52. *See* Heikki Halila, *Oikeudellistuva urheilu*, 19–20 (Helsinki Talentum 2006), and Essi Kinnunen, *Dopingrikos urheilun ja rikosoikeuden leikkauspisteessä*, 11–15 (Helsinki Suomalainen Lakimiesyhdistys 2012).

53. Sports law has close connections to social sciences, for example, questions concerning ethics in sport are also valid in sports law. There are also other developments in society which have to be taken into consideration when applying sports law. Commercialization has a crucial impact on sport and sports law. In this context, it is not difficult to find interesting interfaces between organization and business management, marketing and sports law.

In some cases, it is even possible to oppose any attempt to develop general doctrines of sports law based on the idea that legal governance would destroy sport. In this respect, general doctrines are seen as one precondition for the juridification of sport.

69. It is essential to define the concept of general doctrines when evaluating the general doctrines of sports law. General doctrines are composed of legal concepts, legal principles and legal theories.[54] Legal concepts bridge the gulf between a legal system and social facts. Legal concepts help us to evaluate legal problems. They can be described as lenses because legal concepts make it possible to separate the essential from the unessential. One of the fundamental tasks of legal concepts is to define juridical problems. Legal concepts have a normative basis.

70. There has been some discussion concerning legal concepts in sports law in Finland. Halila has stated that players' rights, transfer fees and ineligibility sanctions are specific legal concepts in sports law.[55] These concepts have a natural connection to the core area of sports law and content which differs from other branches of law.

71. Legal principles have a close connection to different values and goals. Legal principles differ from legal rules when it comes to their content, form and formulation. Legal rules adhere to an either-or logic: they are either applied or not.[56] If two legal rules stand in contradiction, only one of them can be valid and applicable. Legal principles, on the contrary, follow a both-and logic. A conflict between two principles is resolved by weighing both, but neither of them loses its validity or applicability.

72. Legal principles require that the material background (values) on which they are based should be realized as widely as possible. Legal principles can be seen as summaries of the normative contents of a branch of law or the legal order as a whole. In these cases, legal principles function as general legal principles.[57] Furthermore, legal principles can be seen as legal sources supporting legal norms and normative premises for legislative solutions. In this way, these principles create opportunities for evaluating the legal order in a systematic way. Despite this background, they cannot be defined solely on the basis of their normative content; they have close connections to legal order. The question of institutional support is relevant when forming and applying these principles.

54. Kaarlo Tuori, *Ratio and Voluntas. The Tension Between Reason and Will in Law* 173 (Farnham Ashgate 2011).
55. Heikki Halila, *Oikeudellistuva urheilu*, 15–16 (Helsinki Talentum 2006).
56. *See*, e.g., Kaarlo Tuori, *Ratio and Voluntas. The Tension Between Reason and Will in Law,* 190 (Farnham Ashgate 2011).
57. Kaarlo Tuori, *Ratio and Voluntas. The Tension Between Reason and Will in Law,* 189 (Farnham Ashgate 2011).

73. There have been some discussions concerning legal principles in sports law in Finland. According to Halila, two distinct legal principles exist in sports law.[58] The first is the principle of the interest of sport and is closely related to the autonomy of sport: questions and problems related to sport should be dealt with by sports organizations. The second is the principle of the interest of the athlete and concerns the legally protected position of athletes. An individual's freedoms are protected by the legal order, and this background is also relevant in sport.

74. According to Aine, sports law has three general principles: the freedom principle, the fair play principle and the functioning of sports competitions principle.[59] The freedom principle is based on the idea that the individual has a central role in sports. This freedom can be seen as a driving force in sport. There are some fundamental assumptions on which the freedom principle is based. These assumptions concern the position of the individual in modern society and his or her ability to act. At the same time, the relationship between the individual and modern society is defined by these assumptions. It is possible to evaluate these questions from different theoretical perspectives.

75. The freedom principle has many dimensions. Freedom of association is a corner stone of the Finnish legal system. It has several functions in our society. Freedom of association can be seen as a precondition for the functioning of the political system. In sport, the so-called positive dimension of freedom of association is highly relevant. Individuals have a right to form sports associations without a permit, be members of these associations, and participate in the activities of these associations. Correspondingly, individuals have no obligation to be members of sports associations in order to engage in sporting activities.

76. Fair play is a fundamental concept in sport. There are different options to evaluate fair play. A central distinction can be made between formal fair play and informal fair play. Formal fair play is expressed as a norm as regards keeping the written rules of the game.[60] These rules can be characterized as constitutive rules which create the very possibility of playing a game. Fair play is evaluated in this context. No external criteria for evaluation are needed. Written rules stipulate what is an appropriate way of playing a game.

77. There can be some practical challenges for evaluations based on formal fair play. Sports competitions are hardly ever realized in full accordance with the formal rules.[61] Formal rules can be imperfect. Some situations which have relevance

58. Heikki Halila, *Oikeudellistuva urheilu*, 15 (Helsinki Talentum 2006).
59. Antti Aine, *Urheiluoikeuden kantavat periaatteet*, Oikeustiede – Jurisprudentia, 19–23 (2011).
60. *See*, e.g., Johan Steenbergen & Jan Tamboer, *Ethics and the Double Character of Sport*, in *Ethics and Sport*, 39 (M.J. McNamee & S.J. Parry eds, Routledge 1998), and Sigmund Loland, *Fair Play: Historical Anachronism or Topical Ideal?*, in *Ethics and Sport*, 83 (M.J. McNamee & S.J. Parry eds, Routledge 1998).
61. *See* Sigmund Loland, *Justice and Game Advantage in Sporting Games*, in *Values in Sport*, 161 (Torbjörn Tännsjö & Claudio Marcello Tamburrini eds, Routledge 2000).

in practice have not been taken into consideration when forming written rules. Additionally, some written rules can be open to various interpretations. There might be a need to interpret or specify these rules. In these circumstances, it is evident that external material is needed when evaluating fair play.

78. Sport is a wide societal phenomenon which can be evaluated from different perspectives. It seems that the freedom principle and the fair play principle do not cover all the relevant aspects in sport and an additional principle concerning collective and organizational aspects of sport is needed. Sporting activities can be engaged in different ways and different contexts. Individuals can go in for sport independently and by buying some additional services on the market. Organizational requirements are limited in these occasions. However, competitive aspects of sport are present in many cases. Competitions cannot be arranged, by its definition, without other athletes and teams. There might be direct connections between athletes and clubs, but, in most cases, sports competitions are organized by sports federations.

79. The case law of the EU Internal Market Law and Competition Law provides many impulses for constructing the principles of the functioning of sports competitions.[62] However, some distinctions can be found in the relevant case law. The smooth functioning of sports competitions is evaluated as part of the peculiarities related to the relevant context when applying the norms of free movement and competition law. In sports law, the smooth functioning of sports competitions forms an independent basis for legal regulation. Therefore, it is evident that different legal constructions have been used when evaluating the legal relevance of sports competitions and their organizational requirements in various branches of law. Despite these differences, it is essential to identify the material aspects related to the smooth functioning of sports competitions.

80. Legal theories form the third part of general doctrines. Legal theories can help to resolve conflicts and tensions between legal concepts and legal principles. Legal theories can also organize legal principles into a prima facie order of preference. Legal dogmatics has as a central task the ordering of legal principles. It is essential to notice that these tensions between legal principles cannot be resolved *in abstracto* on the basis of legal theories. On the contrary, it is essential to combine legal theories and the facts of each case when applying legal principles. No systematic theories on sports law have yet been presented in Finland.[63] The development of legal theories represents a challenge for this branch of law in the future.

62. *See*, e.g., Case 36/74, *Walrave and Koch v. Association Union cycliste internationale*, ECR 1974 1405, Case C-176/96, *Lehtonen and Castors Canada Dry Namur-Braine v. Fédération royale belge des sociétés de Basketball et Asbl Basket Liga-ligue Basket Belgium*, (2000) ECR I 2681, and joined Cases C-51/96 and 191/97, *Cristelle Deliége v. Asbl Ligue Francophone de judo et disciplines associées*, (2000) ECR I 2549.
63. Antti Aine, *Urheiluoikeuden kantavat periaatteet*, Oikeustiede – Jurisprudentia, 51–52 (2011).

81. It seems reasonable to assume that general doctrines play a central role when systematizing the legal order. A basic distinction can be made between systematization based on formal (consistency) and material (coherency) aspects. The former is inadequate in most cases; systematization should rather be based on material aspects. It is possible to refer to coherency of law. Coherency is also a precondition for material justice in individual cases.

82. Legal principles play a central role when promoting the coherency of law. They also form a solid basis for an independent branch of law. The basic structure of a branch of law can be anchored to the legal order by forming legal principles. Therefore, legal principles are needed in sports law and this is also an obvious choice when systematizing sports law in Finland. Research on the general principles and general doctrines is needed in Finland. Furthermore, this is the only way to improve the legal conditions on which individual cases may be decided. Legal principles are norms which are applicable in legal decision-making.[64] Additionally, legal principles can function as arguments employed in interpreting written sources of law.

64. *See* Kaarlo Tuori, *Ratio and Voluntas. The Tension Between Reason and Will in Law,* 189–190 (Farnham Ashgate 2011).

Part I. Organization of Sports

Chapter 1. Sports Governance

§1. Public Authorities

I. The Ministry of Education and Culture

83. The division of work between the Government, local authorities, sports clubs and federations has a solid basis in the Finnish sports system. On the one hand, sporting activities are mainly organized by sports clubs and federations and, on the other hand, the Government and local authorities have an important role to govern the Finnish sports system. It is a fundamental task for local authorities to provide sports facilities and create favourable conditions for sport and physical activities. The Ministry of Education and Culture is responsible for the overall management, coordination, and development of the national sports policy, and for the creation of favourable conditions for engaging in physical activities. The Ministry's Department for Cultural, Sport and Youth Policy and the Department's Sports Division have the main responsibility for developing and coordinating sports policy. Serving as a panel of experts, the National Sports Council assists the Ministry of Education and Culture when performing its duties.

84. The Ministry of Education and Culture has a coordination body for sport policy (LIPOKO). The body was for the first time appointed on 8 January 2020 for a three-year period from 2020 to 2023. It has a mandate to coordinate governmental efforts to promote physical activity and to find solutions to reduce sedentary lifestyles. Its operation is partly based on previous work by the broad horizontal steering group for health-enhancing physical activity. The ministries' scorecards on physical activity and mobility prepared by the National Sports Council are also guiding the work of the coordination body.

85. There are various mechanisms of governance in the Finnish sports system. The Ministry of Education and Culture can direct sport policy through legislation and financing. The Ministry finances sports in order to promote recreational, competitive and top-level sports in order, among other things, to advance the well-being and health of the population and to support children's and young people's development through sports.

86. The Ministry of Education and Culture grants state aid from the state budget to sports organizations, sport education and research, sports facilities construction, athletes' grants, local sports provision, international sport cooperation and other sports activities. About 90% of the funds are allocated to local sports provision, national and regional sports bodies, liberal education, the construction of sports institutes and sports facilities, and sports research. The rest is used to support performance sports, children's and young people's sports and health-enhancing physical activity.

87. The Government supports the activities of sports federations with some EUR 40 million annually. State funding is one of the main preconditions for the fact that approximately 350,000 children and young people and approximately 500,000 adults can use the services of 7,800 sports clubs and 130 sports federations annually. Traditionally, a clear distinction has been made between sports federations and clubs when allocating the above-mentioned state aids. The Ministry of Education and Culture grants subsidies mainly to national sports federations for various activities in sport. In principle, sports clubs are subsidized by local authorities, who receive annual government grants based on unit costs for the purpose. However, the funding policy is gradually changing and even local sports clubs can currently have subsidies from the Ministry of Education and Culture for certain grass-roots projects.

88. The Government and local authorities have a duty based on the Sports Act (390/2015) to create favourable conditions for sport and physical activity. This can be done, for instance, by providing sports facilities. About 75% of the 30,000 sports facilities in Finland have been constructed and are operated by local authorities. These activities are highly important because private sports facilities, mostly located in major cities, are not available for everyone.

89. As a strategic choice, the Ministry of Education and Culture emphasizes the role of sports and physical activity in enhancing the health and well-being of the population. The Ministry of Education and Culture strongly supports sports and physical exercise targeted at adults, the elderly, and special-needs groups to achieve the beneficial effects of sports on functional capacity, health and well-being.[65] At the same time, one of the priorities is to develop children's and youth sports and sport education.

90. Top-level sport has long traditions in Finland. Therefore, it is evident that the Ministry of Education and Culture promotes top-level sport. One of the current issues concerns the division of work and responsibilities in performance sports. Some measures have been taken to clarify the situation. Financial support is granted for the development of the athlete's career and programmes supporting it. Measures

65. *See also The National Policy Programme for Older People's Physical Activity. Health and Well-Being from Physical Activity* (Publications of the Ministry of Education and Culture 2012:17, Helsinki 2012).

have also been taken to develop scholarship and reward schemes and coaching programmes to enable gifted young athletes to combine a sports career with education.

91. The Ministry of Education and Culture monitors the implementation of ethical principles in sport. An advisory board for ethical questions in sport was established by the Ministry of Education and Culture in November 2015.[66] It functions as a platform for cooperation between sports organizations and the Government when evaluating ethical questions in sport and related international dimensions.

92. The advisory board's objective is to promote fair play in sport and compliance with international conventions related to sport-related ethical issues. It has a mandate on several issues: to monitor and develop the joint activities of the public authorities and the sports movement in matters related to ethical questions; keep track of international cooperative efforts towards the resolution of sport-related ethical problems; make recommendations on sport-related ethical issues to parties affected by them at any given time; serve as a national body for cooperation and coordination between sporting associations, public authorities and the gaming sector in matters regarding prevention of the manipulation of sporting competitions; and also to act in accordance with the Convention on the Manipulation of Sports Competitions as a national action group. The advisory board can make proposals to the Ministry of Education and Culture on reports, studies and development projects as well as issue statements to the Ministry on sport-related ethical issues. It can also draft general principles for national cooperation in the fields/areas of match-fixing, spectator violence, and anti-doping work.

93. The Government supports anti-doping work in Finland. The focus of these activities is on preventing the use of performance-enhancing substances or methods which are harmful to an athlete. Therefore, anti-doping work safeguards an athlete's right to fair play. There is no anti-doping agency operating as part of the Government in Finland. However, the Ministry of Education and Culture promotes anti-doping work and supports the Finnish Center for Integrity in Sports (FINCIS) financially. Sports federations are also responsible for running their own anti-doping programmes. These programmes are regularly evaluated by the Ministry of Education and Culture when granting state aid based on the Sports Act. The Ministry of Education and Culture can steer the development of anti-doping activities in sports federations by increasing and, if necessary, decreasing its financial support to them.

94. Finland is an active partner in international cooperation concerning sports policy. The crucial questions concern, for example, developing legislation and administration, promoting employment and equality, intensifying anti-doping activities, preventing spectator violence, and enhancing athletes' status. The Ministry of

66. https://minedu.fi/en/project?tunnus=OKM038:00/2015 (accessed 18 Nov. 2015).

Education and Culture regularly participates in bilateral, multilateral, and intergovernmental cooperation, as well as, in Nordic cooperation and in EU cooperation. The most important cooperation organizations are the Council of Europe, the EU and UNESCO.

95. Local authorities have a special responsibility for promoting physical activity, health and well-being. Sports provision can be seen as a basic municipal service.[67] The role of local authorities has been recognized in the Sports Act and they receive statutory government aid for these activities. At the same time, local authorities bear most of the costs of local sports provision themselves. A common feature of the recent development has been that the structures and content of municipal sports services have become more varied and differentiated and this has caused challenges for the realization of sport as a basic right. Some steps have been taken to improve the present situation. The continuing structural reform of the municipal and service structures has accelerated the development of the range of municipal services and competence-building. This reform has also encouraged the pooling of resources and participation in cross-municipal cooperation as this can have a positive effect on the possibilities of having equal sports-related services in every part of Finland.

II. Sports Policy in Finland

96. The Finnish government presented a report on sports policy on 25 October 2018. The report forms a solid basis for sports policy in Finland during the 2020s. The scope of the report is extensive: it covers policies to increase physical activity at different stages of life, the construction of sports facilities, civic activity in physical activity and elite sports. The ultimate goal is to significantly enhance people's physical activity. The report has close connections with the resolution adopted by the Finnish government on 11 December 2008, outlining their policy for promoting sport and physical activity. In this resolution, the Government pledged to promote sport as a way of life, and to encourage citizens, organizations and public administration to promote physical activity in Finnish society.

97. Finnish sports culture has different dimensions. It covers not only top-level and competitive sport but also different forms of health-enhancing physical activity.[68] This multidimensional character of sport has expanded the possibilities of using sports policies as tools when promoting the well-being of society. The abovementioned dimensions are also important for individuals: various forms of sport can offer everyone a wide range of opportunities for participation and inclusion. Primarily, physical activity can have a positive effect on the well-being of the population at all stages of life. Physical activity can support the growth and development of

67. *Government Resolution on Policies Promoting Sport and Physical Activity*, 11 (Ministry of Education Publication 2009:44).

68. *Government Resolution on Policies Promoting Sport and Physical Activity*, 9 (Ministry of Education Publication 2009:44).

children and young people; it can also help maintain work and functional capacity, increase the independence and joy for life of older citizens, and add to a sense of solidarity in society.

98. Traditionally, sport has been recognized as an important factor in well-being in Finland and most Finns have a very positive attitude towards sport. However, overall physical exercise at the population level has decreased and individual differences in physical activity have grown during the last decades in Finland. The varied opportunities for sport have only partly been embraced. This context poses a great challenge for public administration because it has a central role in promoting sport. This promotion can be seen as an investment for the future: an increase in physical activity would create remarkable savings in public finances.

99. According to the Government's vision for a national sport policy, Finland is a society where everyone has an equal opportunity to pursue a sportive way of life and to experience communality through sport.[69] Sport is regarded as an essential element in the well-being of an individual and society. The Government emphasizes that the pre-requisites for sport are secured through sustainable choices made by citizens, communities, and society together.

100. The Government is committed to promoting physical activity as a way of life.[70] Realization of this goal requires that opportunities for personal physical activity at various stages in life can be increased, and the preconditions for sports activities that promote participation and communality and nurture comprehensive equality can be improved. In addition, physical activities as an integral part of day-care, school and study days can be promoted, and the operational prerequisites of ethically sustainable competitive and top-level sports can be ensured.

101. Some fundamental choices have to be made when enforcing the Government's vision for national sport policy.[71] First, it is essential to see sport and physical activity as an entity in people's way of life and lifestyles. Second, sports policy must be understood as being part of a welfare policy which concerns all administrative sectors. Third, the priorities in the promotion of physical activity must include the development of favourable conditions, competence-building, and measures to improve the pre-requisites of non-governmental activities. Cooperation also has its strengths in sport.

---

69. *Government Resolution on Policies Promoting Sport and Physical Activity*, 15 (Ministry of Education Publication 2009:44). *See also Sport and Equality. Current State and Changes of Gender Equality in Finland* (Publications of the Ministry of Education and Culture 2012:13, Helsinki 2012).
70. *Government Resolution on Policies Promoting Sport and Physical Activity*, 17 (Ministry of Education Publication 2009:44).
71. *Government Resolution on Policies Promoting Sport and Physical Activity*, 17 (Ministry of Education Publication 2009:44).

102. The Government's aim is to develop Finnish sports culture so as to achieve the following desired conditions covering all phases of life.[72] As a starting point, the importance of children and young people learning the necessary skills for physical activity and adopting a sportive and active way of life should be emphasized. Young adults must be able to maintain physical activity as a way of life after becoming independent and during their studies. The working-age population must be able to engage sufficiently in physical activities for their health and must be increasingly responsible for their own physical activity. The ageing population must maintain their capacity to live an independent life, their functional capacity, intellectual vitality and social interaction through everyday physical activity.

103. According to the Government's vision, it is also important that cross-sector cooperation promoting sport development becomes established, and that the division of labour between different organizations is clarified.[73] Sport must be seen as an integral part of municipal welfare strategies. In this way, sport can be recognized as a basic service in the welfare policy of municipalities. All organizations and actors are important when realizing the Government's vision. Non-governmental organizations must have a stronger role as organizers of sports activities, and their professionalism must be developed. Additionally, the growth of sport-related knowledge and competence of various professional groups should be feasible.

104. The Government has also emphasized that the number of people taking sufficient exercise to maintain health must increase and that the number of those who become marginalized in sport must be decreased in accordance with the aims set in the Government Resolution on development guidelines for health-enhancing physical activity and nutrition (2008:10).[74] At the same time, it is important to notice that the Government's vision also covers other dimensions than recreational sport and the health-enhancing functions of physical activity. The governmental vision has given a clear message to competitive sports, special-needs groups within sport, and the public administration. Competitive and top-level sports must be given more emphasis and the duties of public administration in top-level sports must be clarified. Adapted physical activity geared to special-needs groups will be increased which will require more focused measures, for example, for mobility-impaired people, people with an immigrant background, and the unemployed. The efficiency and effectiveness of the public administration measures must be increased within sport. The only way to achieve these goals is to improve the monitoring and evaluation of policies pertaining to sport.

---

72. *Government Resolution on Policies Promoting Sport and Physical Activity*, 18–19 (Ministry of Education Publication 2009:44).
73. *Government Resolution on Policies Promoting Sport and Physical Activity*, 19–20 (Ministry of Education Publication 2009:44).
74. *Government Resolution on Policies Promoting Sport and Physical Activity*, 21–22 (Ministry of Education Publication 2009:44).

§2. SPORTS GOVERNING BODIES

I. The Model of Sport in Finland

105. There are different models of sport. A basic distinction can be made between the European Sports Model and the American Sports Model.[75] A typical feature of the European Sports model is its pyramid structure. National athletes and players are at the bottom of the pyramid, and national clubs can be seen as associations of these athletes and players. Regional federations are associations of national clubs. Regional federations and sometimes national clubs are members of national sports federations. In practice, there is just one sports federation in one country. National federations form a continental federation. National federations and continental federations are, for their part, members of an international sports federation.

106. The American Sports Model differs from the European Sports Model in many interesting ways. The American Sports Model emphasizes the vertical dimension of sport. This means that connections and relationships between different clubs and organizations on the same level of sport are held to be important. Sports competitions are organized by independent leagues and other organizations. Typically, these sports competitions are not controlled by national sports federations; cooperation in sport is therefore league-orientated. Additionally, commercial factors are of the essence when organizing sports competitions and leagues. The commercial context of sport is very strong in North America. The American Sports Model also includes junior sport. Unlike in Europe, schools play an essential role in the organization of junior sport. Clubs and other associations play a secondary role in junior sport in North America.

107. The organization of sports operations and competitions in North America reflects the American Sports Model. Whereas in Europe, sports leagues are mainly open (promotion and relegation are based on the competitive merits of each team or club), in North America, leagues are closed. Contractual arrangements with a league and other clubs are required when a club wants to join a league. Clubs and teams in the major leagues are considered as franchises.[76] Sport is seen as a product to be sold jointly in North America. A competitive balance between clubs is therefore regarded as essential for business. These aims can be achieved using different methods. Collective labour agreements function as legal mechanisms to organize many important questions relating to the organization of professional leagues. This is a peculiarity of US Antitrust legislation. Collective labour agreements can include, for example, salary caps and draft systems.

75. *See* Lars Halgreen, *European Sports Law. A Comparative Analysis of the European and American Models of Sport,* 64–65 (Kobenhavn Forlaget Thomson 2004).
76. *See* Lars Halgreen, *European Sports Law. A Comparative Analysis of the European and American Models of Sport,* 76 (Kobenhavn Forlaget Thomson 2004).

108. Sport is organized in Finland according to the European Sports Model. The pyramid structure provides many opportunities for creating connections between professional sport, amateur sport and junior sport. There is a question about the vertical dimension of sport. In practice, this can mean solidarity mechanisms which allow transfer of economic resources from the top-elite sport to the grass-roots level. The vertical dimension of sport also concerns promotion and relegation between different leagues and competitions. Open leagues are based on the idea that competitive merits are of utmost importance when deciding matters of promotion and relegation. Leagues and competitions are mainly open in Finland. Additional economic criteria can sometimes be set but this does not alter the basic structure of the mechanism. However, there is one exception to this in Finland: the Finnish Hockey League has set multiple criteria when deciding whether a new team can join the league.

109. The pyramid structure has some disadvantages which must be evaluated within the field of sports law. The pyramid structure leads to highly concentrated sports markets. The structure of one national sports federation per state leads to a de facto monopoly situation which has many consequences. Sports organizations and other federations can often regulate the legal status of their members in a collective manner. This competence is typically based on sport regulations which govern the organization of different sports competitions. These regulations have an immediate effect on the legal status of athletes and other individuals in sport. This effect is intensified by the hierarchical structure of sport. In practice, an athlete has no choice but to accept these regulations if he or she wants to participate in sports competitions. The stronger effects the decisions of sports organizations have on athletes' legal status, the more important it is to evaluate critically the justified scope of freedom of association. These challenges have to be taken seriously in the relevant research in Finland. Legal research can construct models and solutions which can alleviate the problems based on the pyramid structure of the Finnish sports system.

110. There are some special features of sports organizations in Finland. Associations have a strong position in the Finnish sports system. It is possible to say that associations form the core of the sports organization in Finland and their activities have a strong legal basis. Freedom of association is protected by the Constitution of Finland; according to Chapter 1 of the Finnish Association Act (503/1989), an association may be founded for the common realization of a non-profit purpose. Therefore, commercial aspects are not the core area of sports clubs and other associations, but many commercial activities are related to sport in Finland. Commercialization of sport is commonplace, even in Finland, despite some natural limits to this development. The scope of the relevant markets is limited in Finland, and this affects practical business opportunities.

111. In the next sections, the main structures in the Finnish sports system are evaluated. Based on the pyramid structure, it is legitimate to start the evaluation at the top of the national pyramid. The Finnish Olympic Committee (FOC) is the most important national sports organization in Finland because it brings together all the national federations of different sports. At the next level, national sports associations and clubs are discussed. In this context, national sports federations can be seen as forming an association of sports clubs.

II. The Finnish Olympic Committee

112. The FOC has a dual role as a sports governing body in Finland. It was founded in Helsinki on 2 December 1907 and was accepted as a member of the International Olympic Committee (IOC) at the IOC's 9th Session in The Hague. In 2017, the mandate of the FOC changed as a result of the merger of the FSC and the FOC. Therefore, the FOC is also an umbrella organization for FSFs. Altogether, it has eighty-nine members. The FOC has multiple tasks based on its rules. Basically, the FOC looks after the interests of its member organizations by enhancing mutual cooperation, providing services, and serving as a lobbying organization. It also represents Finnish sports organizations in national and international activities in its field.

113. The FOC is an association governed by the Finnish Association Act (503/1989).[77] The board is the highest operative body of the FOC. It has a chairperson, two vice-chairpersons and nine members who are elected at the association's annual general meeting for a four-year term. The FOC has more than fifty full-time employees located at the main office in Helsinki. The Secretary-General represents the highest level of management.

114. The FOC promotes and develops success-oriented and ethically sustainable elite sports in Finland. The core values guiding the activities of the Committee are honesty, transparency and openness, internationality, an athlete-orientation, Finnishness, responsibility, and cooperativeness. The Committee's mandate includes strategies which can enhance the broad success of Finnish elite sports at an international level.

115. The High Performance Unit (HPU), founded in 2013, has a central role in the organization of the FOC. The HPU is leading and developing Finnish elite sports: it directs and coordinates the activities of the national elite sport network, including elite disability sport. The HPU also channels finances, know-how and facilities-related resources to the network. Currently, three programmes (the Sports Academy Programme, the Peak-Phase Programme, and the Research and Development Programme) are run based on these resources. In its work, the HPU has close connections to the Ministry of Education and Culture.

116. Some strategic decisions have been made by the HPU such as those concerning an athlete's path. These decisions describe an athlete's journey from childhood to the peak phase where they engage in elite sport. The HPU has emphasized

77. https://www.olympiakomitea.fi/ (accessed 23 May 2021).

those practical activities which have a positive influence on the training and working conditions of athletes and coaches. These activities can concern different periods of the athlete's path. Strong emphasis has been placed, for example, on providing world-class support and services during the preparation processes for major competitions.

117. The modern Olympic movement has various educational goals and tasks which have been assigned to the International Olympic Academy (IOA). It has a mandate to promote Olympism together with national Olympic academies. The Finnish Olympic Academy (FOA) was founded in 1987 and acts as an expert group of the FOC in the field of Olympic education. The Academy has twelve members who are nominated by the FOC for a period of four years.

118. Annual sessions and the Olympic Education Programme are the main activities of the FOA. Annual sessions function as a platform to promote the fundamental principles of Olympism through discussion between local decision-makers, officials, teachers, coaches, athletes, students and representatives of the arts and sciences. The Olympic Education Programme provides students at elementary and secondary schools opportunities to learn the meaning of fair play, community spirit, and tolerance. This programme can have various forms, for example, schools are encouraged to organize an Olympic Day during the Olympic Games.

119. The choices made by the FOC are based on the common vision of Finnish sports organizations: 'We are the world's most physically active sports nation – 2020.'[78] The strategy of the FOC aims to realize this vision. The initial point of departure for Vision 2020 is a strong commitment to increase the quantity and quality of people's physical activity throughout their entire life. Sports and physical activity have many functions in Finnish sports culture. In practice, they can support an active way of life which can involve, for example, exercising, striving for top performances, as well as maintaining health and well-being. Sports organizations have a duty to ensure that everyone has the opportunity to exercise and participate in sports based on their individual skills and goals.

120. Realizing the above-mentioned vision is a huge challenge both for the FOC and its member organizations. Being the world's most physically active sports nation is a goal that requires concrete steps to be taken without delay. The current activities of the FOC and its member organizations have been evaluated critically and some of these activities have been altered in order to promote more effectively physical activity, sports, and civic activity. However, much more has to be achieved before Vision 2020 is realized. It is a common task that both Finnish sports organizations and public authorities need to work towards in order to reach the goal.

121. The FOC, together with the FINCIS, is a key organization that promotes ethical values in Finnish sports culture.[79] The ethical ideals and goals of fair play

---

78. *The Finnish Sports Confederation, Strategy 2020.*
79. This role was previously carried out by the FSF.

adopted at the FSF General Assembly on 20 November 2010 are still relevant today.[80] The FOC has played an important role in promoting these ideas and goals in sports in Finland. According to the Sustainability Compass at the FOC, the intention is to bring fair play into practice and ensure a value-based culture as well as good governing practices. The core themes are transparency, economic efficiency, non-discrimination and fair play.

122. The ethical ideals and goals of fair play include many important aspects. The fundamental starting point is that everyone is equal.[81] This is true irrespective of our age, gender, place of residence, social standing, health, nationality, mother tongue, ethnic background, religion, sexual orientation or other similar personal traits or life situations. This idea can be summarized as 'treat others as you would like to be treated'. In sport, there are no opponents but only friendly competitors. Sports operations must be based on mutual trust, as well as the laws and statutes that are in place.

123. It is also important to emphasize that everyone has the right to participate in sports and physical activities.[82] Equality, diversity, and fairness can be seen as the foundations of the Finnish sports community. Finnish sports organizations want to develop a diverse environment and atmosphere through active dialogue with all parties and organizations interested in sports and physical activities.

124. Educational aspects are always present in sport. In practice, there is an educational aspect to every event and situation related to sports and physical activities (e.g., training, games, tournament trips, volunteer events and parents' nights).[83] According to the Fair Play Handbook, we are all educators and we educate through example. The primary motivator must always be the best interests of children and young people. It should be emphasized that each and every person should be encouraged to continue learning throughout their lifetime in the context of sports and physical activities.

125. Sports operations must promote health, safety and well-being: there is no room for drugs and violence within the sphere of sports and physical activities.[84] Intervention is required and help must be provided in cases where there are physical or psychological problems, and sports organizations must work actively to

80. *Fair Play Handbook. Working ahead to More Ethical Sports and Physical Activities* (Finnish Sports Federation 2010).
81. *Fair Play Handbook. Working ahead to More Ethical Sports and Physical Activities*, 10 (Finnish Sports Federation 2010).
82. *Fair Play Handbook. Working ahead to More Ethical Sports and Physical Activities*, 12–13 (Finnish Sports Federation 2010).
83. *Fair Play Handbook. Working ahead to More Ethical Sports and Physical Activities*, 15–17 (Finnish Sports Federation 2010).
84. *Fair Play Handbook. Working ahead to More Ethical Sports and Physical Activities*, 18–20 (Finnish Sports Federation 2010).

prevent such cases. A safe environment for sports and physical activities has to be created. In practice, anti-doping work is an essential part of sports operations in Finland.

126. Environmental questions are part of everyday life in sport.[85] Finnish sports organizations must preserve our shared environment, as well as advise others on how to do so. Together, sports organizations can develop to be more respectful of nature and search for a balance between sports activities and sustainable development. Finnish sports organizations should participate in endeavours that will lead to a cut in carbon emissions.

127. Decision-making in sport must have a democratic basis.[86] In decision-making procedures, Finnish sports organizations must carefully plan and listen, as well as explain the reasoning behind each decision. Cooperation is an inexhaustible resource in the Finnish sports system. The rules used in the decision-making process should be available to everyone. Crimes and misconduct need to be taken very seriously by sports organizations. However, sports organizations must believe in people and be willing to give everyone a second chance. Additionally, Finnish sports organizations must manage their finances so that they have both realistic and sustainable basis.

128. Sports federations govern disciplinary procedures in Finland. Typically, every sports federation has a disciplinary board. Disciplinary sanctions are imposed by each board based on sports federation's internal rules and codes. There are some challenges related to the above-mentioned system. Sports regulations and disciplinary rules typically cover matches and other sports competitions but not training sessions or other activities where violent incidents commonly occur. Traditionally, all forms of violence have been evaluated in disciplinary proceedings based on a vague concept of unsportspersonlike conduct. It is evident that offences should be more precisely described in disciplinary codes to fulfil the requirements of legal certainty. Additionally, sanctions based on a sports federation's disciplinary code are valid within that sport and they do not have effects in other sports. Therefore, an athlete or a coach who has been sanctioned in one sport is free to engage in sporting activities and work in other sports unless otherwise stated in a disciplinary code.

129. In order to avoid the above-mentioned challenges, a specialized disciplinary board was established under the FOC in May 2021. The disciplinary board has a mandate to consider all severe emotional violence and unethical behaviour cases in Finnish sports. The mandate covers also training sessions and other activities not related to sports competitions where violent incidents can occur. The disciplinary code enforced by the specialized disciplinary board describes precisely the relevant offences, and unsportspersonlike conduct is just one of the offences mentioned in

85. *Fair Play Handbook. Working ahead to More Ethical Sports and Physical Activities*, 21–23 (Finnish Sports Federation 2010).

86. *Fair Play Handbook. Working ahead to More Ethical Sports and Physical Activities*, 25–27 (Finnish Sports Federation 2010).

the code. This is highly important to fulfil the requirements of legal certainty. The sanctions imposed by the disciplinary board are applicable to different sports.

130. Accepting the board's mandate is voluntary so each sports federation has to accept the board's mandate. It remains to be seen how many sports federations are willing to change their internal rules. Based on negotiations during the preparation process, it is likely that most sports federations will do so. This would be an important step towards ensuring a safe sports environment for all athletes, irrespective of their age.

III. National Sports Federations

A. Introduction

131. The national sports federations are the key players in the Finnish sports organization. In practice, they are associations governed by the Finnish Associations Act. Members of the national sports federations are sports clubs; these federations can therefore be seen as associations of the sports clubs. The national sports federations representing sports clubs are also members of the international sports federations and are part of the pyramid structure peculiar to the European Sports Model. Most of the national sports federations are also members of the FOC.

132. There are some differences in the organizational structures of national sports federations in Finland: some federations have a distinct district level in their organizations, while others do not. A common feature of national sports federations is that they organize competitions and other sports operations nationwide, grant competition licences, and have the authority to impose disciplinary sanctions. These activities are partly funded by the Ministry of Education and Culture based on the Finnish Sports Act (390/2015), but it is worth noting that athletes and sports clubs also fund these sports operations. Additionally, national sports federations tend to have various sponsors and other partners.

133. In practice, national sports federations are differentiated in Finland in terms of their organization and sports operations. In the following, only a few examples can be mentioned and evaluated. These examples concern national sports federations which differ on the basis of the scope and scale of their sports operations and, therefore, give a good impression of the organizational structures of sport in Finland.

134. One of the traditional sports federations in Finland is the Finnish Athletics Federation (SUL) which was established in 1932.[87] The emphasis of the Federation's operations is on achieving international success at the top level of athletics and developing pluralistic athletics activities for children, young people, and adults. Additionally, they provide services for recreational athletes. The services related to

87. www.yleisurheilu.fi (accessed 26 Jul. 2023).

competition and coaching are offered to people of all ages, either directly by the Federation or through the member clubs. In practice, these services are provided via the Federation's 21 district organizations for more than 600 athletics clubs and the approximately 70,000 people involved in athletics in Finland.

135. The SUL has a board with eleven members who are in positions of trust. It is the highest operative body of the Federation, elected by the Federation Council for a two-year term. The Council comprises representatives from the district organizations and special groups that are members of the SUL. The Federation has over twenty full-time employees, including the Managing Director who represents the highest level of management. The organization of the Federation is divided into member services and top-level athletics operations, as well as competition, information and marketing activities, and financial and administrative tasks. The SUL is a member of the International Association of Athletics Federations (IAAF).

136. Ice hockey is the most popular sport in Finland. The Finnish Ice Hockey Association (SJL) which was established in 1929 organizes sports competitions and ice hockey operations in Finland.[88] It is a member of the International Ice Hockey Federation (IIHF). Based on its popularity, the organizational requirements for sports operations in ice hockey are huge in Finland: there are over 72,000 registered ice hockey players, 430 ice hockey clubs, and over 3,000 teams. Every season, approximately 40,000 games are played in the 223 ice halls with 260 rinks in Finland.

137. The SJL has eight district organizations into which the member clubs are divided. The council comprises representatives from the district organizations and special groups that are members of the SJL. The board is the highest operative body of the Association and it has nine members who are elected by the Association's council for a two-year term. The Association has more than fifty full-time employees located in the eight area divisions and the central office in Helsinki. The Managing Director represents the highest level of management. The organization of the Association is divided into sports administration and sports operations.

138. The Finnish Volleyball Association founded in 1959 is one of the largest national sports federations in Finland.[89] It is also a member of the International Volleyball Federation (Fédération Internationale de Volleyball, FIVB). The Finnish Volleyball Association has approximately 700 member clubs. Altogether, there are over 118,000 volleyball players in Finland. The number of registered players is over 12,200, of whom approximately 7,200 are junior players. There are over 1,400 teams playing in the series organized by the Association. Men play in seven and women in six series levels and, in addition, there are many regional and local series.

139. The Finnish Volleyball Association has a board of nine members, who are elected by the Federation's council for a two-year term and who are the highest

---

88. www.finhockey.fi (accessed 26 Jul. 2023).
89. www.lentopallo.fi (accessed 26 Jul. 2023).

operative body of the Association. The Council comprises representatives from the district organizations and special groups of the Association. The Association has over fifteen full-time employees, including the Managing Director, who represents the highest level of management. The organization of the Association is divided into information and marketing activities, area services and sports operations, and top-level sports operations.

B. Disciplinary Rules and Regulations

140. National sport federations have the mandate to enforce sport regulations. Disciplinary rules and regulations are applied in cases where sport regulations have been breached. Disciplinary rules and regulations should have a valid legal basis.[90] It is not relevant just to refer to the autonomy of sport in this respect. In the legal context, the autonomy of sport does not form a solid legal basis for disciplinary proceeding, although disciplinary rules and regulations serve to ensure that the objectives of sport are attained. This perspective is evident when taking into account the effects which disciplinary sanctions have on the legal positions of individual athletes, coaches, and officials.

141. In fact, sports organizations have a wide competence when governing individual athletes, coaches, and officials. Disciplinary rules and procedures form a core area of this competence. The juridification process in sport has enhanced the importance of this dimension. Additionally, the commercialization of sport has also had similar effects because economic interests related to sport have become stronger.

142. Discussion on the legal basis for disciplinary proceedings has a close connection to the legal regulation of associations. However, the freedom of association should not form a valid legal basis for these proceedings without qualifications. There are several legal questions which are relevant in this respect.[91] First, it has to be evaluated against whom the discipline sanctions may be imposed and what is the concrete legal basis for these sanctions. Second, it is essential to elaborate which body is competent to impose disciplinary sanctions and what kind of actions can be sanctioned in the discipline proceedings. Third, it has to be evaluated what kind of sanctions can be imposed in disciplinary proceedings and how legal protection is carried out in these proceedings.

143. There are several factors which can be relevant when evaluating requirements for the legal basis for disciplinary proceedings. In practice, disciplinary proceedings can concern professional sport, competitive sport, as well as recreational sport. It has to be elaborated whether the relevant context of sport can affect the

90. *See also* Olli Rauste, *Urheiluoikeus*, 710–711 (Helsinki Lakimiesliiton Kustannus 1997).
91. *See also* Risto Riitesuo, *Erottaminen ja kurinpitomenettely yhdistyksessä*, 13–14 (Helsinki Lakimiesliiton kustannus 2001).

above-mentioned requirements.[92] Additionally, it is worth evaluating whether the severity of the disciplinary sanctions has an effect on these legal requirements.

144. Disciplinary sanctions can be imposed by national sports federations and individual sports clubs based on their internal rules and codes.[93] In practice, sports federations have the competence to impose disciplinary sanctions on a national level if nothing else has been decided or agreed. However, it is possible that a sports federation can, based on a contractual arrangement, transfer this competence to an entity which organizes sports operations in a tournament or a league. Most of these cases concern a relationship between a sports federation and a sports league, which is governed by a mutual cooperation agreement. It is essential that the competence of a sports league to impose disciplinary sanctions is properly defined in the cooperation agreement.

145. The crucial legal question concerns how athletes, coaches, teams, and other entities can be considered to be subject to the sports federation's disciplinary power. The scope of the personnel application of disciplinary rules and regulations can be evaluated legally from different perspectives.

146. It is possible to construct a nexus of rules as the legal basis for disciplinary proceedings. In this legal construction, athletes, coaches, and other persons are members of a sports club, which is, for its part, a member in a sports federation. In practice, there should be provisions in the rules of both the sports club and the sports federation on the disciplinary proceedings and their competence to issue disciplinary sanctions on individuals and other entities. Under this condition, the nexus of rules forms a solid legal basis for disciplinary proceedings and sanctions.

147. If the nexus of rules is unbroken, the competence to issue disciplinary sanctions cannot be challenged by athletes or other entities. This legal construction is also valid in the context of professional sport.[94] However, the nexus of rules construction has a minor relevance in professional sport because, in most cases, there are contractual arrangements between athletes and sports clubs.

148. Contractual arrangements between an athlete and a sports club provide an alternative legal basis for disciplinary proceedings. Typically, it is a question of provisions in an employment contract by which a player or an athlete commits himself to follow and respect the sports regulations and disciplinary code of a sports federation or a league. This provision cannot be seen as unexpected or unfair from the athlete's perspective. Regularly, these provisions have been applied to player agreements in Finland.

---

92. *See also* Heikki Halila, *Oikeudellistuva urheilu*, 362 (Helsinki Talentum 2006).
93. *See also* Risto Riitesuo, *Erottaminen ja kurinpitomenettely yhdistyksessä*, 104–105 (Hel sinki Lakimiesliiton kustannus 2001).
94. Heikki Halila, *Oikeudellistuva urheilu*, 368–374 (Helsinki Talentum 2006).

149. In some cases, the contractual basis for disciplinary proceedings is not connected to employment contracts between an athlete and a sports club. In these cases, it is typically a question of provisions in contracts concerning the athlete's payment, attendance in national teams or sponsorships. From the legal perspective, it is essential that an athlete has given his commitment to accept the competence of a sports federation of a league to issue disciplinary sanctions.

150. In many practical situations, an athlete's commitment to follow and respect sports regulations and the disciplinary code of a sports federation is legally constructed by the fact an athlete has purchased a sports licence, which is a precondition for participating in competitions and tournaments. This construction has some weaknesses with regard to the legal basis for disciplinary proceedings. It is possible, at least in individual cases, that an athlete is not de facto aware of all the provisions of the sports licence. This is highly likely at least when an athlete has not personally bought the licence. Therefore, it is essential to inform all the athletes of the relevant provisions. However, at least in professional sport, athletes should be aware of all the typical conditions of sports licences.

151. Additionally, it is interesting to evaluate whether the fact that an athlete has participated in sports competitions can lead to a de facto commitment to disciplinary proceedings. In the legal context, it is a question of a tacit expression of the individual's will or consent.

152. In Finnish case law, the conditions for participating in a sports competition have been evaluated as an adhesion contract in which the binding effect can be based on the athlete's awareness of the provisions or established practices of the sport.[95] From the legal point of view, awareness of all the relevant details concerning disciplinary proceedings can be problematic if an athlete is not well informed because the scope of these proceedings can be difficult to estimate in advance without sufficient information. An athlete or other person has to know in advance all the relevant details concerning his commitment. This perspective is enhanced by the fact that disciplinary sanctions can be severe.

153. Occasionally, disciplinary sanctions are overruled in appeal procedures. In these cases, the fact as to whether an employer is entitled to have compensation when his employee has been suspended from matches without a legal cause should be elaborated further. This question is theoretically interesting but, in fact, it can be difficult to receive compensation in these cases in Finland. A very important precondition for these claims is that there is a contractual relationship between an employer and a sports federation or a sports league. Otherwise, special requirements based on the Finnish Tort Liability Act (412/1972) have to be met because the damage suffered concerns, in most cases, economic loss.[96] According to Chapter 5, section 1 of the Act, damages shall constitute compensation for economic loss

95. KKO 2002:38.
96. *See*, e.g., Pauli Ståhlberg & Juha Karhu, *Suomen vahingonkorvausoikeus*, 322–324 (6th ed., Helsinki Talentum 2013).

that is not connected to personal injury or damage to property only where the injury or damage has been caused by an act punishable by law or in the exercise of public authority or, in other cases, where there are especially weighty reasons for the same.

IV. National Sports Leagues

154. A common feature of top series or leagues in Europe is that they are organized by an independent sports league. Typically, this arrangement is based on an agreement between a national sports federation and a league. Such agreements include, for example, disciplinary procedures, organizational rules of the game and sports operations. Additionally, a sports league can make by-laws concerning the transfer of player rights and other questions related to sports competitions. A league and its owners can also make other contractual arrangements which are relevant to the organization of sports operations.

155. The establishment of distinct sports leagues can be evaluated within the context of the commercialization of sport. A league as an organizational choice, gives elite clubs an opportunity to directly influence sports operations and competition systems. There are four major sports leagues in Finland. The Finnish Hockey League was established in the 1970s and is responsible for organizing the top-level national ice hockey series in Finland. Based on every indicator, the Finnish Hockey League is the largest sports league in Finland, but it has some competitors: the Finnish Football League (established in 1990), together with the Finnish Ball Association, organizes the top-level football series in Finland; Superpesis Ltd. (established in 1991) is the organizer of the national Finnish baseball league; and SSLB Salibandy Ltd. organizes the top series for men and women in floorball.

156. A sports league can be organized in many parallel ways. The legal background is of relevance when deciding organizational questions concerning a sports league. A sports league can be organized as an association in accordance with the Finnish Association Act. The Finnish Football League is a good example of this kind of association. An association may be established only for the common realization of a non-profit purpose, which means, in practice, that the economic activities of a sports league can only be run for non-profit purposes. The distribution of the assets of an association to its members is not legally possible, although contractual arrangements can be made between an association and its members. In the context of sports leagues, the importance of top-level management has been emphasized. The board is a central organ in an association, but there are no legal norms relating to a managing director or a commissioner in the Finnish Associations Act. These arrangements, which are important in sports leagues, must be based on the rules of an association.

157. A sports league can be organized as a limited liability company. In Finland, the Finnish Hockey League, Superpesis and SSBL Salibandy are limited liability companies governed by the Finnish Limited Liability Companies Act. The profits of a limited liability company may be distributed to the shareholders. The managing director is an organ of a limited liability company and has the general competence to oversee the executive management of the company. Relations between different shareholders can be organized according to the Articles of Association or contractual arrangements. As a legal construction, a limited liability company has many advantages when organizing a sports league, it is therefore not surprising that most of the sports leagues in Finland are organized in this way.

158. The organization of a sports league is not solely based on whether a league is an association or a limited liability company. A cooperation agreement between a sports league and a national sports federation is also very important in this respect.[97] It defines the mutual rights and obligations of the parties. Relevant factors may include, for example, the right to award the national championship title and quality criteria for the organization of sports operations in a league. Based on the European Sports Model, it is evident that a national sports federation requires a sports league to commit itself to respecting the rules and regulations of an international sports federation.

159. The competence to regulate sports operations can in practice be shared in different ways. The key question concerns the qualification of teams for a league. This has to be decided on the basis of contractual provisions between a league and a sports federation. There can be both competitive and economic evaluation criteria, and these are typically based on different licensing systems. Additionally, there can be clear provisions in the cooperation contract about how to decide the number of teams that are to play in a league, competitive systems (regular/play-off season) and schedules.

160. Disciplinary regulations form an important part of the contractual relationship between a league and a sports federation. The crucial question concerns which party has the competence to take disciplinary action and how its legal basis can be defined. It has been rare in Finland that sports leagues have had the independent competence to issue disciplinary sanctions. The Finnish Hockey League is an exception because it has a wide competence in this respect and has its own disciplinary organization.[98] This arrangement is based on a cooperation agreement between the league and the SJL.

161. In some cases, the disciplinary code of a national sports federation is also applicable in a league and disciplinary sanctions can be issued either by a disciplinary body of a league or a sports federation. Occasionally, sanctions given by a sports league can be based on a shareholders' agreement. Various economic sanctions can be defined in advance in a shareholders' agreement concerning different violations of sport rules and by-laws. Additionally, there can be provisions in the Articles of

97. *See also* Olli Norros, *Urheiluliigan organisointi*, 148–149 (Helsinki WSOYpro 2011).
98. https://www.liiga.fi/fi/liiga/kurinpitosaannot (accessed 3 May 2021).

the Association which are also relevant in disciplinary proceedings. However, these provisions cannot form a legal basis for sanctions directly concerning the employees of the shareholders.

162. There may be other questions which are relevant to organizing sports operations in a league and which have to be decided in a cooperation agreement, for example, sports officials and costs relating to officiating. Commercially, it is important to decide how to share media rights between a national sports federation and a league. Occasionally, the national sports federation is willing to transfer these rights to a league.

163. Finnish sports leagues have different competencies to run sports operations. The Finnish Hockey League has wide competence to organize sports operations. It has a strong and independent organization to carry out all necessary operations, including both ice hockey operations and administrative and marketing operations. The Finnish Hockey League also sells all the commercial rights related to the league. The Finnish Football League is an association of elite football clubs but it has only a limited competence to run the relevant sports operations. The Finnish Ball Association has a strong mandate in this respect. The core task of the Finnish Football League is to sell the league's commercial rights. The situation is more or less the same in relation to Superpesis and Salibandyliiga.

V. Sports Clubs

164. Sports clubs are at the bottom of the pyramid structure of the European Sports Model. In most cases, members of sports clubs consist of athletes and other individuals. In practice, grass-roots sport is organized by sports clubs in Finland; altogether there are over 7,800 sports clubs. Membership of a sports club is often a precondition for participating in sports competitions.

165. Sports clubs are associations governed by the Finnish Association Act (503/1989), and may be founded for the common realization of a non-profit purpose. A sports association can have sections and other functional entities. Members play a central role in decision-making in associations. Decisions concerning the admission of members are taken by the executive committee unless the rules state otherwise. In principle, every member must have an equal legal position and rights in the decision-making procedures. Members exercise their power of decision at the meetings of the association.

166. Every association must have an executive committee which must carefully attend to the affairs of the association in compliance with the law, the rules, and resolutions adopted by the association. Members of the executive committee are liable to pay compensation for all damage they have either wilfully or negligently caused to the association. The same applies to damage caused to any member of the association or a third party by an act against the Finnish Associations Act or the rules of the association.

167. There are many reasons why an association is an ideal organization for sports clubs. Sports clubs can be seen as associations of their members whose purpose is to ensure opportunities to participate in sporting competitions and engage in recreational sporting activities. Despite this background, there may be some legal challenges relating to the organization of activities in associations governed by the Finnish Association Act. Unlike the Limited Liability Companies Act (624/2006), there are no provisions concerning situations of negative equity. This can be problematic at least in cases where professional sport is run by an association and when its competitors are limited liability companies. This is a question of a level playing field between competitors.

168. Whereas an association is regarded as an individual legal person, teams, sections and other functional entities are not. This can be a relevant distinction when evaluating the legal status of obligations made by teams or sections and the liability of an association in relation to these obligations.

169. The Finnish Supreme Court considered these questions in a case concerning an association whose sections were not individual legal persons according to the Finnish Association Act.[99] In this association, there was an established practice of persons acting for different sections by taking loans and making other commitments in their own names. Funds which were gained in this way were used to finance the activities of the sections. In practice, all the debts were paid back by the association and were entered in the balance sheet as obligations of the association.

170. In the case, the plaintiff had paid over EUR 38,000 on behalf of one of the sections of an association. He claimed that the association was responsible for these payments. He stated that he had acted in the belief that the association would take care of the payments and he had only signed the promissory notes for that reason. The plaintiff claimed that the association had breached these obligations and had therefore wilfully caused him damage. For its part, the association claimed that there was no contractual arrangement between the association and the plaintiff concerning these debts. Furthermore, since the executive committee of the association had made no decision concerning the debts, the association was not legally responsible for the debts.

171. The Supreme Court, giving its ruling on 14 July 1999, stated that the relevant question in the case was whether the person acting on behalf of the section or the association was responsible for the debts. It was indisputable that the debts were incurred and used to finance the activities of the section. Furthermore, it was indisputable that the executive committee of the association had not made any decision concerning these debts. The executive committee had the sole competence to make any decisions concerning the obligations of the association. Sections were not individual legal persons even though they had independently organized their own activities.

99. KKO 1999:85.

172. The Supreme Court stated that there were two separate structures – the formal one and the practical – for making decisions on debts and other obligations in the association. The formal structure was based on the rules of the association. The executive committee of the association had the sole competence to make all the decisions. However, in practice, persons acting for the sections were obliged to sign and accept obligations in their own names based on the fact that the legal structure and the decision-making procedures of the association did not work properly. These debts and other obligations were regularly considered in the association as obligations of the sections and not of the persons acting for them. Funds of the sections were also used to repay these debts.

173. The Supreme Court stated that the executive committee was aware of these practical arrangements, and it did not take any action to change them. The plaintiff had incurred the debts on the understanding that ultimately, the association was responsible for repaying the debts. In these circumstances, the plaintiff's expectation that the association was responsible for the loan was legitimate. The Court ruled that the association must compensate the plaintiff for all the losses caused by its actions.

174. The case shows that relationships between an association and its sections must be organized in a systematic way.[100] An association is responsible for obligations in all of its activities if there is a solid legal basis for these. In practice, there can be many unclear questions and procedures in associations in this respect, and these must be dealt with in a pro-active way. There is a pressing need to have so-called compliance programmes which may help to prevent difficult problems occurring in associations.

175. The importance of this pro-active perspective was also emphasized in the Supreme Court's ruling on 27 April 2015.[101] The case concerned a sports club which was an association governed by the Finnish Association Act (503/1989) and which had several sections as functional units. One of the sections took care of the football teams in the club. There were some disagreements between the football teams and this section, and as a result of these disagreements, nine of the ten teams in the section and some players from the other team decided to change to another sports club and represent it in the sports competitions.

176. The key question in this case concerned the legal status of funds raised by each of the teams for their own sports activities after they changed to another club. The funds were raised through voluntary work and payments made by players and their parents, and the levels of these payments were decided by each team. The funds were in the accounts of each team and all of them had their own treasurer. However, the funds were included in the balance sheet of the sports club. After the transfer to the other sports club, the teams and players asked for the funds because

100. *See also* Heikki Halila, *Oikeudellistuva urheilu*, 340–342 (Helsinki Talentum 2006).
101. KKO 2015:34.

they had raised the funds, not the sports club or the section. The sports club rejected this request and stated that it was not the members but the association as a legal person that was entitled to these funds.

177. The Supreme Court stated in its decision that an association may obtain rights, make commitments and appear before a court of law or other authority as a party if it has been registered in accordance with the provisions of the Finnish Association Act. A registered association is a legal person which has its own funds. If an association holds a bank account, there is a presumption that the funds in the account belong to the association.

178. An association has the competence to regulate its internal activities and functions. This competence is based on the freedom of association guaranteed in section 13 of the Constitution of Finland.[102] In the *travaux préparatoires* of the Finnish Association Act, it has been emphasized that, in this context, an association has broad competence to decide how its internal activities and procedures are organized in order to realize its purposes as defined in its rules.[103] This competence, which forms the core of the freedom of association, must not be restricted by the discretionary norms of the Finnish Association Act. It has been stated in the case law that the organization of internal activities and procedures can be legally evaluated based on practices which are permanent and de facto approved by the association.[104]

179. In clarifying its decision, the Supreme Court argued that the case was not based on the right of the players to the funds, but rather on the legal question of whether the teams that had changed to other sports clubs were functional units which were entitled to funds in their accounts. In deciding this question, it was not relevant whether the players in question were members of the sports club.

180. The Supreme Court stated in its decision that the teams that had changed to another sports club were not themselves legal persons and could not obtain rights. However, it has been emphasized in the *travaux préparatoires* of the Finnish Association Act, as well as in the legal literature, that functional units that are not legal persons can have in their possession funds and other property which are deemed to be for the realization of purposes of these units.[105]

181. Based on the freedom of association guaranteed in the Constitution of Finland, an association can decide how financial management is internally organized and how the competence of different functional units, like teams, is defined in this respect. Normally, these questions are decided in the rules, by-laws and decisions of an association. Additionally, practices which are permanent and de facto approved by the association are relevant.

102. *See* KKO 2013:81, 3, KKO 2012:50, 10, and KKO 2008:41, 7.
103. HE 64/1988 vp, 15.
104. KKO 1999:85.
105. Heikki Halila & Lauri Tarasti, *Yhdistysoikeus*, 725–726 (4th ed., Helsinki Talentum 2011).

182. The Supreme Court stated that even a functional unit that does not qualify as an unregistered association as defined in sections 58 and 59 of the Finnish Association Act can have funds specially allocated to its activities and under its control. However, there are certain criteria for these functional units in this respect. It is essential to evaluate how well-established the functions of this unit are and how wide the competence of this unit is, as it has been defined in the rules and practices of the association, to control relevant funds. It is typical for sports associations to have funds that have been raised by the members for the realization of a non-profit purpose of a functional unit. Additionally, it is relevant to evaluate whether, after the change, the functional unit continues to realize the same non-profit purpose for which the funds are raised.

183. In this case, there was no evidence about how the fundraising and other related practical procedures of each team were regulated by the rules of the sports association or the section in question. Neither had given any relevant instructions. In these circumstances, the legal status of each team and the funds must be evaluated on the basis of the internal practices of the sports association.

184. The case concerned junior teams whose composition was not permanent, but these teams could not be defined as occasional temporary joint ventures either. Rather, these activities and the funding of the teams were organized based on age groups over several seasons which were typical for junior teams. Additionally, the fact that each team had its own treasurer and other officials indicates that the activities were well-organized. These activities were also run independently and were not actively controlled by the sports association or the section in question.

185. The decisions relating to opening the accounts and issuing rights to use these accounts were made by each team. However, the accounts were opened in the name of the sports club and were taken into its balance sheet. The Supreme Court stated that these factors favoured the conclusion that the sports club should be entitled to the funds. However, there were also other factors which have to be taken into consideration when evaluating the relevant legal questions. These questions concerned the purposes for which the funds were raised and the relevant practices relating to how the fundraising and other organizational procedures of each team were regulated by the sports association and the section in question.

186. The funds were raised by voluntary work and payments made by players and their parents. The relevant funds were raised by each team for their own sports activities, and they were collected and assigned only for this purpose. There was no evidence that other actors or organs than the teams and their officials could have made decisions about the funds or that the sports club had the competence to use these funds for other than the above-mentioned purposes. This conclusion was supported by the fact that it was stated at the board meeting of the sports club on 30 November 2008 that the funds should be transferred with the teams to the new sports club. The fact that the sports club rejected this request afterwards does not change this conclusion.

187. In its ruling, the Supreme Court stated that the rules of the sports association and the section in question did not regulate how the fundraising and other related practical procedures of each team were supposed to be organized. Neither had the association given any relevant orders. On the contrary, the sports club had allowed and also contributed to practices which gave each team an independent position to decide how the funds could be used. When the funds were collected and assigned only for special purposes, and each team had broad powers to control these funds, the teams changed to a new sports club and had the right to use these funds. This conclusion is not challenged by the fact that the teams had an opportunity to use different services provided by the sports club.

Chapter 2. Public Regulation

§1. Act on the Promotion of Sports and Physical Activity

I. Introduction

188. Public governance of sports is based on the Act on the Promotion of Sports and Physical Activity (390/2015) (the Sports Act) in Finland. The scope of the Sports Act is very wide. The objective of the Act is to promote opportunities for various demographic groups to engage in physical activity; the well-being and health of the population; the maintenance and improvement of the capacity for physical activity; the growth and development of children and young people; civic action in the field of physical activity, including club activities, top-level sports; integrity and ethical principles in the context of physical activity and top-level sports; and greater equality in sports and physical activity. The efforts to achieve these objectives are based on the principles of equality, non-discrimination, social inclusion, multiculturalism, healthy lifestyles, respect for the environment and sustainable development.

189. Different legislative strategies can be chosen when governing sport and issues related to it. In this respect, a basic distinction can be made between interventionist and non-interventionist legal systems. Finland belongs to the group of non-interventionist legal systems. Neither athletes' rights and duties nor relationships between athletes and sports organizations are defined in the Sports Act. Practical decisions have to be made in sports organizations and athletes' organizations. Therefore, the crucial starting point is freedom of association in this respect. However, there are specific regulations concerning the position of sports and athletes in legislation, for example, the Athletes' Accident and Pension Security Act (276/2009). Additionally, there are sport-specific regulations in certain legal acts, for example, tax legislation.

190. The Sports Act sets out provisions on the promotion of physical activity and top-level sports, the responsibilities of and cooperation between central and local government, the government administrative bodies and the funding to be provided by the state in the field of sports and physical activity. Aside from the provisions of the Sports Act, Finland has to comply with its international obligations under the relevant treaties. Finland has signed various international treaties concerning sport, including international anti-doping treaties.

191. Some key concepts are defined in the Sports Act. For the purposes of the Act, physical activity means spontaneous and structured physical exercise excluding top-level sports. Top-level sport refers to extensive, goal-oriented sports activities aiming at international success. Physical activity promoting health and well-being means all types of physical activity in the course of human life designed to maintain and improve the state of health and functional ability of the population.

II. Organization

192. There are different official organizations responsible for sport in Finland. Section 4 of the Sports Act concerns the state's responsibility. The Ministry of Education and Culture is responsible for the overall management, coordination and development of national sports policy, and for the creation of favourable conditions for engaging in physical activity. This responsibility is based, among other things, on the Constitution of Finland and the Government Act (175/2003).[106] Responsibility for local administrative duties rests with the Regional State Administrative Agencies. More detailed provisions on these duties must be made by government decree. When performing the duties defined herein, the state must, as appropriate, engage in cooperation with municipalities, non-governmental organizations and other actors in the field of physical activity and sport. These organizations and actors can, for example, be sports associations and private undertakings producing services in sport.[107]

193. Section 5 of the Sports Act concerns the local government's responsibility in sport. Responsibility for creating opportunities and facilities for engagement in physical activities at the local level rests with the local authorities. Local government must provide opportunities and facilities for physical activity by providing physical exercise services and organizing physical activities that promote general health and well-being with due regard to the various target groups, supporting civic action including club activities and constructing and maintaining facilities for physical activity. The services mentioned in section 5 can be provided by a local authority organization or in collaboration with local sports clubs and business undertakings.

194. The previously mentioned duties have to be performed in the municipality in collaboration with the various fields of activity by developing local, inter-municipal and regional cooperation and, where necessary, providing for other forms of activity in response to local conditions and needs. In making key decisions on issues related to sports and physical activity, local authorities are required to consult the residents as part of the obligation under section 27 of the Local Government Act (365/1995) to provide the local residents with the opportunity to participate and exert their influence. Local authorities are required to evaluate the residents' level of physical activity as part of the promotion of health and welfare referred to in section 12 of the Health Care Act (1326/2010).

195. Whenever a local authority carries out the activities mentioned in the Sports Act, it cannot engage in market competition unless such services are provided on a commercial basis with commercial goals. Based on this legal background, there is an interesting relationship between section 5 of the Sports Act and Chapter 4a of the Competition Act (948/2011) which concerns securing neutral competitive conditions between public and private sector undertakings. According

106. HE 190/2014 vp, 26.
107. HE 190/2014 vp, 26.

to section 30a of the Competition Act, if a business practice or organizational structure is applied to the economic operations of a municipality, association of municipalities, the state or an entity under their control, which, in the supply of goods or services, distorts or is capable of distorting the conditions of sound and effective competition; prevents or is capable of preventing the creation or development of sound and effective economic competition; or contradicts the requirement of market-based pricing as stipulated by section 66a of the Local Governments Act (365/1995), the Finnish Competition and Consumer Authority must, primarily through negotiations, seek to eliminate such a business practice or organizational structure.

196. There are exceptions in the scope of application of section 30a of the Competition Act. According to section 30b of the Act, what is provided under section 30a cannot apply if the business practice or organizational structure immediately follows from legislation, or if its application would prevent the performance of a major obligation related to citizens' welfare, security or other such common interest. It seems that section 5 of the Sports Act refers to this exception mentioned in section 30b of the Competition Act.[108] However, the exact scope of section 5 of the Sports Act remains to be decided in forthcoming case law. It seems that exceptions to the main rule must be limited by their scope and, therefore, it is not a question of total exclusion of the Competition Act in these cases.

197. There are sports councils both at the national and regional levels in Finland. Section 6 of the Sports Act concerns the National Sports Council. Serving as a panel of experts assisting the Ministry of Culture and Education, the National Sports Council is appointed by the Government for the duration of the parliamentary term. The Council is called upon to address major issues of fundamental importance related to sports and physical activity and, in particular, evaluate the impact of government action in the field of sports and physical activity; submit initiatives and make proposals to develop sports and physical activity; and issue opinions on the allocation of state appropriations for sports and physical activity within its purview. The Council includes sections responsible for the preparation of the issues to be addressed. More detailed provisions on the duties, composition and appointment of the National Sports Council must be made by government decree.

198. Section 7 of the Sports Act regulates Regional Sports Councils. Serving as a panel of experts at the Regional State Administrative Agencies, the Regional Sports Council is to be appointed by the Regional Council. More detailed provisions on the duties, composition and appointment of the Regional Sports Council must be made by government decree.

108. *See also* HE 190/2014 vp, 28.

III. State Funding

199. The Government has a central role to support sports and physical activity in municipalities. Provisions on the central government transfers to local government for the purpose of covering the operating costs of sports and physical activities are set out in the Act on the Financing of Education and Culture (1705/2009). All central government transfers must be used for the activities specified in section 5 of the Sports Act.

200. Section 9 of the Sports Act concerns funding to support the physical activities organized by the regional administration. The Ministry of Education and Culture must allocate appropriations to finance the physical activities organized by the State Administrative Agencies. The use of these funds must be subject to agreement with the State Administrative Agency involved. Additionally, the Ministry may allocate other appropriations to the Regional State Administrative Agencies to be distributed as grants.

201. Government also financially supports organizations promoting sports and physical activity. The conditions for eligibility for state aid to organizations promoting sports and physical activity are set out in section 10 of the Sports Act. To qualify for state aid, an organization promoting sports and physical activity must first be approved as eligible for such aid by the Ministry of Education and Culture. Approval for eligibility may be granted to a registered association whose purpose is to promote sports and physical activity and whose activities are in compliance with the objective specified in section 2 of the Sports Act. When assessing eligibility for state aid, due consideration must be given to the type, extent and social impact of the activities that the association is engaged in, and the ways in which the association promotes equality and non-discrimination.

202. Of the individual sports federations, only one national federation may be approved as eligible for state aid for each given sport. Only federations that operate under the auspices of an international organization or competition system and sport that is of national importance can qualify for state aid. When assessing a federation's eligibility for state aid, due consideration must be given to the type, extent and social impact of the activities that the federation is engaged in, the ways in which the federation promotes equality and non-discrimination, and the extent to which it complies with the ethical principles of sports and physical activity and the international regulations binding on Finland.

203. The Ministry of Education and Culture may withdraw its approval if the federation fails in two consecutive years to meet the criteria for state aid pursuant to the Sports Act or other regulations. This is a new section in the Sports Act. It is based on the need to govern organizational changes in the structure of sport in Finland. More detailed provisions on the criteria for approval of new organizations within the meaning of section 10 of the Sports Act for eligibility for state aid and the procedures to be followed in such approval may be made by government decree.

204. Section 11 of the Sports Act includes appeal procedures for decisions made in state aid cases. A review of the decision of the Ministry of Education and Culture referred to in section 10 above may be requested from the Ministry as provided in the Administrative Procedure Act (343/2003). A decision issued in response to the request for review may be appealed as provided in the Administrative Judicial Procedure Act (586/1996).

205. The granting of state aid to organizations promoting sports and physical activity is governed by section 12 of the Sports Act.[109] The government budget must include an annual appropriation for subsidizing the activities of organizations promoting sports and physical activity. Central government transfers and aid referred to in the Sports Act are financed primarily from Veikkaus Ltd's (the Finnish National Lottery Company) profits from betting, pools and lotteries.

206. According to section 12 of the Sports Act, except for special reasons, a new organization cannot be eligible for state aid until it has operated as a registered association for a minimum period of two years. When assessing eligibility for state aid, due consideration must be given to the type, extent and social impact of the activities that the organization is engaged in, the ways in which the organization promotes the objective of the Sports Act and the ethical principles of sports and physical activity, the extent to which it complies with the international regulations binding on Finland and how it promotes equality and non-discrimination. Operating expenses incurred in the course of business operations are not included in the operating expenditure applied as one of the criteria for granting aid. More detailed provisions on the criteria for granting state aid within the meaning of section 12 of the Sports Act may be issued by government decree.

207. Sports and physical activity facilities are partially funded by the Government in Finland. According to section 13 of the Sports Act, the government budget must include an annual appropriation for granting aid for establishing sports and physical activity facilities and associated recreational facilities. State aid is granted for the construction, acquisition, renovation and refurbishment of sports and physical activity facilities designed to serve the needs of a wide range of user groups. Additionally, aid may, on special grounds, be granted for the construction of other physical activity facilities. These facilities concern, for example, tennis halls, floorball halls and other sports halls which are designed for use of one sport only.[110]

208. Aid for sports and physical activity facilities is granted to municipalities or joint municipal authorities or an entity under their executive control. Aid may also be granted to other entities if such aid is necessary for the attainment of the objectives of the Sports Act. Provisions on the central government transfers to local government referred to above are set out in the Act on the Financing of Education and Culture.

---

109. Further provisions on state aid in addition to s. 12 and s. 14 of the Sports Act are to be found in the Act on Discretionary Government Transfers (688/2001).

110. *See also* HE 190/2014 vp, 31.

209. Section 14 of the Sports Act concerns state aid for other purposes conducive to sports and physical activity. The government budget has to include an annual appropriation for the purpose of granting aid and stipends for research and development in the field of sport and health sciences, research and development projects related to the construction of sports and physical activity facilities, the activities of entities engaged in sports and health science, the provision of information on sports and physical activity, education, international cooperation, the promotion of top-level sports, topical cooperation and development projects in the field of sports and physical activity and other activities referred to in section 2 of the Sports Act.

210. According to section 15 of the Sports Act, the Ministry of Education and Culture is the state aid authority in respect of the aid referred to in sections 8–14. The Regional State Administrative Agency must serve as the state aid authority in respect of aid granted for construction except in the case of high-cost projects and in granting the appropriations to the government agencies referred to in section 9 of the Sports Act. The division of powers between the state aid authorities may be defined in greater detail by government decree.

211. The Sports Act entered into force on 1 May 2015 and repealed the previous Sports Act (1054/1998). There are various transitional provisions in the Sports Act. The Ministry of Education and Culture must review the eligibility for state aid of the organizations that have received aid under the previous Sports Act without any special application. More detailed provisions on the assessment of eligibility for state aid and related procedures may be made by government decree. The National Sports Council in office at the time when the Sports Act entered into force must serve out its term. The terms of the Regional Sports Councils in office at the time when the Sports Act entered into force, expired at the end of 2015. Where the term would have otherwise expired before this time limit, it was nevertheless extended until the end of 2015.

§2. Criminal Liability

I. General

212. It is typical for sport that violations of sports regulations and rules are sanctioned in internal procedures. Rule violations in sport can also be sanctioned by other means than discipline proceedings. In some cases, it has to be considered whether criminal law sanctions can be applied in sport. These cases concern violence in sport. In the legal context, it has to be evaluated in which cases criminal law sanctions should typically be applicable. This is the only way to ensure that the application is coherent in individual cases.

213. Generally, violence in sport receives the most publicity when it concerns elite sport or professional sport. In Finland, this perspective was realized, for example, in the widely publicized ice hockey case in September 2012 where there was a fight on the ice in a training match between two Finnish elite clubs (HIFK and Jokerit). This case and its side effects were discussed widely in the Finnish media and even in the Parliament of Finland. However, violence can also be a problem in other contexts of sport (e.g., recreational sport and junior sport). Additionally, it has to be remembered that violence can be a problem in Finland even in other sports and can have different forms (e.g., spectator violence).

214. The different parts and levels of sport are interrelated. Therefore, a single case concerning professional sport can have side effects, for example, in junior sport. Likewise, every decision made in the disciplinary proceedings on these cases can have similar effects. Basically, the crucial question concerns the prohibited and acceptable ways of playing different games and engaging in sporting activities. These effects should not be underestimated although relevant contexts are often differentiated.

215. Violence in sport can be evaluated from the perspective of the value basis of sport. In legal literature, the relevance of the general principles of sports law has been emphasized.[111] These general principles define the fundamental values and aims of sports law, and therefore, form a solid normative basis for sports law. At the same time, these principles provide a perspective for an evaluation of concrete legal issues concerning acceptable and prohibited ways of engaging in sporting activities. They can be used when applying legal norms and solving legal problems in the field of sports law.

216. The freedom principle and the fair play principle are relevant when evaluating violence in sport. The freedom principle is based on the idea of an individual's central role in sports law. Individuals can use their freedom by participating in different competitions and sporting activities. Violence in sport, in fact, restricts these freedoms and jeopardizes their reciprocal nature. A central task of law is to ensure that individuals can use the freedoms guaranteed under the legal order in an appropriate way in sport. In practice, this can, for example, refer to disciplinary proceedings and educational systems in sport.

217. The freedom principle has close connections with the organization of sport. Individuals can organize and form different organizations in order to support sporting activities. Sports clubs and federations have an essential role when organizing sporting activities. It is also important from a legal perspective that sports clubs and federations can actually function independently and according to their internal goals. Freedom of association is protected in section 13 of the Finnish Constitution. This legal context is relevant when evaluating different options for governing violence in sport.

218. Sport and sports law are based on certain core values. Fair play is the most important value in sport. Everyone should have an equal opportunity to participate in sporting activities. From this perspective, violence in sport can be seen as a lack

111. *See* Antti Aine, *Urheiluoikeuden kantavat periaatteet*, Oikeustiede – Jurisprudentia 1, 19–23 (2011).

of respect for other athletes and teams. Gaining an advantage in sporting competitions by using artificial or unethical methods is prohibited. Formal and informal rules governing sport must not be overlooked when engaging in sporting activities.

219. The general principles of sports law open up a broad perspective for sports and sports law. These principles form a starting point for evaluating the relationship between sports law and other branches of law (e.g., criminal law). These relationships should be evaluated in a systematic way, and this is a question of consistency and coherency. The evaluation may be based on a balancing of different legal principles.

II. Governance Structures in Sport

220. Sport, and activities related to it, can be governed legally and socially in parallel ways. These governing structures form a unit that has to be known when evaluating violence in sport. A basic distinction can be made between internal and external governing structures. Furthermore, the external mechanisms can be divided into public law and private law.

221. Self-governance has long traditions in sport. It is, at least in most cases, flexible and specific features of each context can be taken into consideration in its application. Self-governance is mainly based on disciplinary rules and regulations sanctioned by sports federations. It is obvious that decisions made in disciplinary proceedings have preventive effects. Decisions concerning elite sport or professional sport also have wider effects in recreational sport and in junior sport. Despite the different contexts, these decisions carry a message concerning the acceptable ways of playing a game.

222. Internal governing structures are not only based on disciplinary rules and regulations. It is worth noticing that contractual arrangements can also be effective in governing violence in sport. Provisions in player agreements can be mentioned as an example of an effective internal governing structure in this respect. These provisions can lead to a reduction of a player's payment following an ineligibility sanction decision made in disciplinary proceedings. In practice, these provisions significantly strengthen the factual consequences of decisions made in disciplinary proceedings.

223. Internal governing structures are not only based on punishment and sanctions. It is of the utmost importance that different educational operations are made to influence the attitudes of athletes and their coaches towards violence in sport. Typically, a change in functions and sub-cultures takes time but, at the same time, results achieved in this way form a solid basis for sustainable development in sport. This development concerns the legitimacy of the governing structures and their goals among the athletes, their coaches, and other officials in sport.

224. Violence in sport is governed most efficiently by internal mechanisms. However, this initial starting point does not preclude options to govern violence in sport by external mechanisms. Violence in sport can be governed by criminal law sanctions (e.g., Chapter 21, section 5, Assault, or section 6, Aggravated assault, of the Criminal Code of Finland). These sanctions are legitimate, at least, in the most serious cases. There are some typical features in these cases (an act without any connection to the game, a conscious effort to injure the health of another by breaking the rules of the game, and serious consequences to another's health). In practice, the different aspects of each case have to be taken into consideration when making decisions concerning the criminal law sanctions.

225. Public authorities, especially the Ministry of Culture and Education and local authorities, are important financiers of sport in Finland. Based on this position, public authorities can govern sporting activities despite the freedom of association having a central role in sport. The competence of the Ministry of Education and Culture to govern sporting activities is largely based on the state subsidies granted to national and regional sports organizations. According to section 12 of the Sports Act (390/2015), when assessing eligibility for state aid, due consideration should be given, *inter alia*, to the ways in which the organization promotes the objective of this Act, and the ethical principles of sports and physical activity.

226. In practice, sporting activities are governed by the provisions of the state subsidies. Typically, these provisions have concerned commitment to anti-doping codes and programmes. In some cases, there have been discussions on the possibilities of issuing a decision ordering the discontinuation of the payment of a discretionary state subsidiary and the clawing back of a transfer or part of a transfer already paid. These cases have been concerned with some major anti-doping violations. It is essential to evaluate whether it is a question of a single violation or a large and systematic series of violations. In principle, it would be possible to make the above-mentioned decision also in a case concerning violence in sport.

227. Public authorities are not the only external organs or actors having a significant influence on sporting activities. The significant scandals related to violence in sport have shown that in Finland sponsors and other commercial partners are very sensitive to violence in sport. In practice, this means that they are not willing to cooperate with sports which have a negative public image. Violence is one of the key factors which can affect this image. The practical effects of this phenomenon are huge because sports clubs and other organizations are, typically, dependent on sponsors and commercial partners. However, it is evident that the importance of this de facto governance will not be diminished. On the contrary, business undertakings and other commercial entities will be even more careful with their business image; as their image will not be strengthened by cooperating with sports clubs and athletes involved in violence in sport.

III. Criminal Law Sanctions

A. Legal Basis

228. In the Finnish legal system, criminal law sanctions are mainly based on the Criminal Code (39/1889). Cases concerning violence in sport are mainly evaluated based on the relevant sections of Chapter 21 (Homicide and bodily injury), in the Criminal Code of Finland. According to section 5, a person who employs physical violence on another or, without such violence, injures the health of another, causes pain to another or renders another unconscious or in a comparable condition, must be sentenced for *assault* to a fine or to imprisonment for a maximum of two years. If in the assault, grievous bodily injury or serious illness is caused to another or another is placed in mortal danger, or the offence is committed in a particularly brutal or cruel manner, or a firearm, edged weapon or other comparable lethal instrument is used and the offence is aggravated also when assessed as a whole, the offender must be sentenced for aggravated assault (section 6) to imprisonment for a minimum of one year and a maximum of ten years. If the assault, when assessed as a whole and with due consideration to the minor significance of the violence, the violation of physical integrity, the damage to health or other circumstances connected to the offence, is of a minor character, the offender must be sentenced to a fine as for a petty assault (section 7).

229. Engaging in sporting activities can, in some unfortunate occasions, lead to the death of another athlete or person or bodily injury or illness to another athlete or person. According to section 8, Chapter 21 (Homicide and bodily injury), the Criminal Code of Finland, a person who through negligence causes the death of another must be sentenced for negligent manslaughter to a fine or to imprisonment for a maximum of two years. If in negligent manslaughter, the death of another is caused through gross negligence, and the offence is also aggravated when assessed as a whole, the offender must be sentenced for grossly negligent manslaughter (section 9) to imprisonment for a minimum sentence of four months and a maximum of six years. According to section 10, Chapter 21 (Homicide and bodily injury), the Criminal Code of Finland, a person who through negligence inflicts no insignificant bodily injury or illness on another must be sentenced for negligent bodily injury to a fine or to imprisonment for a maximum of six months. If in the negligent bodily injury, the bodily injury or illness is inflicted through gross negligence, and the offence is also aggravated when assessed as a whole, the offender must be sentenced for grossly negligent bodily injury (section 11) to a fine or to imprisonment for at most two years.

B. Case Law

230. There have been various cases in the case law of the Finnish Supreme Court where the Criminal Code of Finland has been applied in the context of sport.

These cases have concerned various situations and they can be systematized in different ways. In some cases, sections concerning negligent manslaughter and negligent bodily injury have been applied.

231. There is at least one judgment of the Supreme Court which is a classic example of a precedent which concerned negligent manslaughter in the context of physical education.[112] A teacher was nominated as a supervisor for a visit made by comprehensive school students to a swimming pool and the teacher failed to supervise that all the students had come out of the swimming pool after the session. Unfortunately, one of the students was drowned after the swimming period has expired. The Supreme Court stated in its decision that the teacher had, through negligence, caused the death of the student and sentenced the teacher to negligent manslaughter.

232. One decision of the Supreme Court concerned negligent manslaughter in a rally race.[113] A rally car was run off the road at a special stage with the consequence that the co-driver died. The driver was summoned before a court of law on a criminal charge concerning negligent manslaughter. The charge was dismissed because it was not shown that the driver had acted against those standards of diligence and caution which were justified in the actual situation.

233. The Supreme Court has also evaluated negligent manslaughter in a diving training camp.[114] One of the divers was drowned after missing the route during a diving tour. The relevant safety instructions and practices approved by the Finnish Divers' Federation were not followed during the dive. The diver who was killed had considerable general experience in diving but lacked all the required experience for diving in caves. In these circumstances, the diver had consciously breached the safety regulations and other relevant regulations by taking part in the cave diving. All the charges for negligent homicide against the responsible organizer of the diving were dismissed.

234. There are several decisions in the case law of the Finnish Supreme Court in which violence in sport has been evaluated from the perspective of the Criminal Code of Finland. Interestingly, most of these cases have been concerned with ice hockey matches. In one of the decisions, the Supreme Court evaluated a lower division senior ice hockey game during which a player had, after the referee had blown his whistle to stop play, delivered a check to the body of his opponent.[115] The check was delivered with both hands on the hockey stick and no part of the stick on the ice. The check knocked the opponent onto the ice and the player then swung his stick into the face of the other opponent with the consequence that the opponent lost three teeth.

---

112. KKO 1977-II-11.
113. KKO 1982-II-21.
114. KKO 1997:73.
115. KKO 1996:74.

235. The Supreme Court stated that ice hockey is a fast sport. Typically, obstructing an opponent from moving about the ice freely and checking are part of the game. However, ice hockey matches are conducted according to the official rules approved by the IIHF. These rules are aimed at, among other things, ensuring safety and preventing injuries in ice hockey games. The Supreme Court stated further that by engaging in ice hockey games, players can be constructed to accept the possibility that they can have minor injuries during games, even if those injuries are caused by actions against the rules of the game. Therefore, only those actions which differ markedly from the normal flow of the game are evaluated in the context of the Criminal Code of Finland.

236. The Supreme Court stated that swinging a stick at an opponent who is lying on the ice is something which is not part of the nature of ice hockey. Therefore, it was an action which the opponent should not have had to take into consideration in advance. In the relevant case, the referee of the game gave testimony as a witness. He told the court of the law that the actual injury occurred two or three seconds after the play had been stopped. The player had had time enough to stop playing. In these circumstances, the injury could be seen as intentional. The player should have understood when swinging his stick into the face of his opponent that the blow would probably cause physical injury to his opponent. The player had caused the above-mentioned physical injuries deliberately. The Supreme Court sentenced the player to a fine for assault.

237. Violence in an ice hockey match was also evaluated by the Supreme Court in a subsequent decision.[116] Similar to KKO 1996:74, this case concerned a lower-division senior ice hockey game. A player had delivered a check to the neck of his opponent with both hands on the stick and no part of the stick on the ice, with the consequence that it caused a concussion of the brain and other injuries to the opponent.

238. The Supreme Court took into consideration the context of the game when applying the Criminal Code of Finland in the case. The Supreme Court stated that the player had crossed all justified borders by his actions when exercising such power in ice hockey. The player should have understood when delivering a check to the neck of his opponent that the blow would probably cause physical injuries to his opponent. The Supreme Court sentenced the player to a fine for assault.

239. The above-mentioned cases form the core area of the Supreme Court case law concerning violence in sport. There are various cases before the district courts and courts of appeal in this respect; however, these cases are mainly consistent with the Supreme Court case law. Most of the cases concern ice hockey, which is probably a consequence of the nature of the game. Based on the relevant case law, some conclusions can be drawn.

---

116. KKO 1997:129.

240. In the context of the Criminal Code, the rules of each game can be seen as a starting point when drawing a line between the prohibited and the acceptable. It is worth noticing that breaching the rules of the game does not necessarily lead to criminal law sanctions. Only actions which are not related to the flow of the game or are against the spirit of the game and, therefore, cannot be regarded as so-called normal violations of the sporting rules are sanctioned by the Criminal Code of Finland. However, the facts of each case have to be taken into consideration when making legal evaluations and decisions.

241. A typical feature of an act which is sanctioned by the Criminal Code of Finland is that it has been committed after play has been stopped or the match time has been expired. Therefore, the act has no connection to the flow of the game. In a criminal law context, it has to be evaluated whether the act enhances the justified goals of the game. For example, criminal law sanctions are justified when the act is attributed to a player or an athlete who is not playing the ball or the puck and who has no possibility to play the ball or the puck. In these cases, the opponent should not have an obligation to take these actions into consideration in advance.

242. There are different standards to evaluate what acts are punishable in the criminal law context. An athlete can only be asked to give his or her consent to injuries based on actions which are usual in a particular sport and, therefore, predictable.[117] Generality forms one aspect of legal discretion. It has to be evaluated whether an athlete has reached the average standards of conscientiousness in any actual situation. Criminal law sanctions are not justified if an athlete has acted as a decent and cautious athlete. The relevant context of the sport (e.g., professional sport or junior sport) has to be taken into consideration.

243. The fact that athletes sometimes lose their temper in sports competitions is one aspect which is often heard when evaluating violence in sport.[118] It is possible to argue, for example, that an assault is based on an unintentional act. This argument is not legally justified in most cases. The key point concerns what the athlete, who is facing criminal charges, should have understood in the actual situation. In most cases, an athlete should understand that his actions would probably cause physical injuries to his opponent.

244. One peculiar feature of violence in ice hockey concerns the legal responsibility of coaches for actions on the ice. In the criminal law context, it is a question of instigation. According to section 5, Chapter 5, the Criminal Code of Finland, a person who intentionally persuades another person to commit an intentional offence or to make a punishable attempt of such an act is punishable for incitement to the offence as if he or she were the perpetrator.

117. *See* Essi Kinnunen, *Rangaistava toisen vahingoittaminen urheilussa*, 48–51 (Opetusministeriö, Kulttuuripolitiikan osaston julkaisusarja 10/1999, Helsinki 1999).

118. *See also* Essi Kinnunen, *Rangaistava toisen vahingoittaminen urheilussa*, 103–106 (Opetusministeriö, Kulttuuripolitiikan osaston julkaisusarja 10/1999, Helsinki 1999).

245. In practice, an initiative to commit a crime can come from a coach who is trying to strengthen the position of his team in a single match and defeat the opposing team. In commercial sport, an innocent wish of a coach can be relevant when players are playing for their future contracts. However, simply having a tolerant attitude towards playing hard and using methods situated in the grey area of ice hockey does not meet the above-mentioned criteria of the Criminal Code of Finland. Nevertheless, a coach should be able to understand that his actions can lead his players to employ physical violence on other players. A coach should understand the causal link between his act and the offence committed by his player. In junior sport, the responsibility of a coach for his team should also be underlined when applying the above-mentioned section.

IV. Conclusions

246. Violence in sport is a serious problem that should not be overlooked from a legal or social perspective. The whole structure of sport, as well as relationships between different parts and levels of sport, need to be understood when evaluating violence in sport. It is evident that this problem does not only concern professional sport. On the contrary, decisions made in this respect in professional sport can produce signals of how violence is to be generally evaluated in sport. Therefore, individual decisions in top-elite sport are important when counteracting violence in sport. Additionally, it has to be remembered that violence can have different forms in sport. Even in Finland, these problems do not only concern ice hockey although ice hockey has a central role in the relevant case law.

247. Governing and controlling violence in sport is a multidimensional phenomenon. Governance should primarily be based on the internal structures of sport. Disciplinary proceedings and different contractual arrangements offer, at least in most individual cases, workable solutions to reduce violence in sport. However, it is of utmost importance that these internal mechanisms are applied in a coherent way. Public proceedings are needed when the offences are severe as in individual cases or when the problems are extensive.

248. Individual cases and their details receive the most publicity in public discussions on violence in sport. This is understandable because of the role of the media. However, a different dimension or approach is needed when deciding how to use public mechanisms to govern and control violence in sport. The scope and regularity of the phenomenon have to be taken into consideration when making decisions concerning legal and other social governance on violence in sport. This is the only way to have a solid basis for future decisions.

§3. Dispute Solution in Sport

I. Introduction

249. In sport, various decisions are made which have effects on the legal positions of athletes, coaches, other persons, and sports clubs. These decisions can concern, for example, discipline codes, sports operations, and the organization of sports. It is a typical feature in sports that athletes, clubs, and other organizations are de facto obliged to follow the above-mentioned decisions if they want to engage in sporting activities within an organized sport. This situation results from the regulatory competence that sports federations and other sports organizations have implemented based on the European Sports Model.

250. In the above-mentioned circumstances, the requirements for legal protection are of utmost importance. Everyone has the right to have a decision pertaining to his or her rights or obligations reviewed by a Court of Appeal or other independent organ of the administration for justice. In practice, it is a question of effective protection of legal rights in sport and, especially, the right of appeal.

251. There are three basic legal mechanisms for dispute solutions in sport in Finland. Two of these mechanisms are based on the Finnish legislation. First, disputes concerning sport and sporting activities can be dealt with before the general courts (District Courts, Courts of Appeal, and the Supreme Court). Second, any sports dispute in a civil or commercial matter, which can be settled by agreement between the parties, may be referred for a final decision to one or more arbitrators. Additionally, there is an internal procedure for dispute solutions in the Finnish sports system. The Finnish Sports Arbitration Board can consider disputes related to sport within the limits of its rules. The Finnish Arbitration Board has no legal status in the Finnish legislation. Therefore, the competence of the Finnish Sports Arbitration Board is only based on its rules which are approved by sports federations and other sports organizations.

II. General Courts and Arbitration

252. Sports clubs have a central position when organizing sport in Finland. Sports clubs are typically associations governed by the Finnish Association Act (503/1989). An association may be founded for the common realization of a non-profit purpose. It can make various decisions that have an effect on its members' legal positions. These decisions can concern, for example, diminishing the special benefits that a member according to the rules enjoys in an association, discipline sanctions, or expulsion from an association.[119]

---

119. According to s. 14 of the Finnish Association Act, an association may expel a member on the grounds stated in the rules. Nevertheless, the association invariably has the right to expel a member

253. The Finnish Association Act provides specified legal mechanisms concerning how to challenge decisions made by the association before a general court. Section 32 of the Finnish Association Act concerns the rights of any member, the executive committee, or any member of the executive committee of the association to bring an action against the association in order to have a resolution declared void. A member, the executive committee, or any member of the executive committee of the association may bring an action against the association to have a resolution declared void in cases where a resolution of an association has not been conducted in a proper manner or if it otherwise is contrary to the law or the rules of the association. However, a person who has contributed to the adoption of the resolution at the meeting has no right to bring an action for annulment.

254. An action as mentioned in section 32 of the Finnish Association Act can be based on both material and procedural grounds. The material grounds for an action to be declared void concern situations where a resolution is contrary to the law or the rules of the association. However, it has been stated in the legal literature that an action can even be based on the unfairness of the resolution.[120] In these cases, section 36 of the Contracts Act (956/1982) is applied. According to this section, the term may be adjusted or set aside if a contract term is unfair or its application would lead to an unfair result. In determining what is unfair, regard must be given to the entire contents of the contract, the positions of the parties, the circumstances prevailing at and after the conclusion of the contract, and other factors. The rest of the contract may also be adjusted or declared terminated if a term referred to in the above-mentioned paragraph is such that it would be unfair to enforce the rest of the contract after the adjustment of the term. A provision relating to the amount of consideration must also be deemed a contract term.

255. Section 32 of the Finnish Association Act can involve various procedural problems for associations as regards decision-making practices. One example of a relevant procedural aspect that can be mentioned is the failure to hear a member before a decision is made. Section 15 of the Finnish Association Act, states that before a decision to expel a member is taken, the member concerned must be granted an opportunity to give an explanation concerning the matter, except where the reason for expulsion is failure to pay the membership fee.

256. According to section 32 of the Finnish Association Act, the action has to be brought within three months of adopting the resolution, or, if the resolution has been adopted without a meeting, i.e., by organizing the votes via post or electronic or technical means, then within three months of the date of the record concerning the resolution. If no action is brought within the time limit, the resolution is to be

---

who has failed to fulfil the obligations to which he or she has committed himself or herself by joining the association, and by his or her action within or outside the association has substantially damaged the association or no longer meets the conditions for membership laid down by law or the rules of the association.

120. *See* Heikki Halila, *Oikeudellistuva urheilu*, 230 (Helsinki Talentum 2006).

deemed valid. If the executive committee of the association has brought an action, a meeting of the association must be convened without delay in order to elect a representative to act for the association.

257. Resolutions taken by an association can have, at least in some occasions, adverse effects on a third party. A specified legal remedy has been established in the Finnish Association Act for these situations. Notwithstanding any action for annulment, a resolution must be considered void if it violates the rights of a third party. Subject to section 27(3), a resolution must likewise be considered void if it diminishes the special benefit that a member according to the rules enjoys in the association or if its contents or the procedure following its adoption essentially violates the equality of a member. Any member, of the executive committee, or any member of the executive committee of the association may bring an action against the association to have a resolution of the association confirmed as being void.

258. The fact that an action has been brought against a resolution made by an association may have legal consequences in the legal status of that resolution based on section 34 of the Finnish Association Act. When an action has been brought against an association, the court may ban the enforcement of a resolution of the association or order that it be interrupted. Such a ban or order may also be lifted. The above-mentioned resolution may not be appealed against separately.

259. The pyramid structure of the European Sports Model enhances, in practice, the position sports federations have in disciplinary proceedings. Most of the disciplinary proceedings are run by sports federations. In the context of the Finnish Association Act, it is worth elaborating whether an athlete can base his actions on section 32 or 33 when challenging, before a general court, a disciplinary decision made by a sports federation. This question was relevant in a case decided by the Supreme Court: the main question concerned a professional athlete's right to have a disciplinary decision made by one FSF in a doping case dealt with before a general court.[121]

260. The athlete in question was not a member of the sports federation but was a member of a sports club that in turn was a member of the sports federation. The Supreme Court stated in its decision that, in these circumstances, the athlete had no right to base her actions on section 32 of the Finnish Association Act. Resulting from this conclusion, the only way to have legal protection under the Finnish Association Act was to refer to section 33, which concerns third parties. However, the Supreme Court concluded that the athlete could not be seen as a third party in this case because the athlete had actually declared herself to be bound by the rules of the sports federation. Therefore, the Supreme Court dismissed all the claims based on section 32 and section 33 of the Finnish Association Act.

---

121. KKO 1998:122.

261. The Supreme Court stated further that resolutions of associations can be legally evaluated before a court of law on other than sections 32 and 33 of the Finnish Association Act; the Court mentioned that these grounds would only be in exceptional circumstances because freedom of association is protected in section 13 of the Constitution of Finland. However, the Supreme Court concluded that these exceptional circumstances can be linked to sufficient need for the legal protection of an athlete.[122]

262. Based on the above-mentioned legal construction, the Supreme Court dealt with the case, but only concerning whether the ground for the ineligibility sanction was justified. The Supreme Court stated that the ineligibility sanction had justified ground in this case. By contrast, the Supreme Court did not deal with the claims based on the unreasonable nature and practical consequences of the ineligibility sanction. These claims can only be evaluated based on sections 32 and 33 of the Finnish Association Act because there was not sufficient need for the legal protection of an athlete in this respect.

263. The above-mentioned decision of the Finnish Supreme Court can be seen as justified. On the one hand, the decision has a solid legal basis. An ineligibility sanction has evidently adverse effects on a professional athlete's right to earn his/her livelihood by the employment, occupation, or commercial activity of his/her choice. The freedom to engage in commercial activity is protected in section 18 of the Constitution of Finland. On the other hand, the decision can be evaluated in the context of juridification of sport in Finland. The need for legal protection of athletes, or at least professional athletes, has to be taken seriously into consideration when making decisions in anti-doping cases. At the same time, the decision enhances the opportunities for athletes to have their cases dealt with before a court of law because the three-month time limit based on section 32 of the Finnish Association Act does not concern cases fulfilling criteria mentioned in the decision.

264. Sports organizations, sports clubs, athletes, and other actors sign various contracts in sport. General courts can deal with disputes relating to these contracts and agreements as civil cases. Alternatively, parties in a single case can sign an arbitration agreement.[123] According to section 2 of the Finnish Arbitration Act (967/1992), any dispute in a civil or commercial matter, which can be settled by agreement between the parties, may be referred for final decision to one or more arbitrators. It may also be agreed that such disputes, which in the future arise from a particular legal relationship specified in the agreement, must be finally decided by one or more arbitrators unless otherwise provided for in statutory law.

265. One of the crucial questions that have to be decided concerning disputes in sport is whether a valid arbitration agreement has been made. According to section

122. *See also* Markus Manninen, *Missä urheiluriidoissa urheilija pääsee Suomessa yleiseen tuomioistuimeen?*, 40–45 (Turun yliopiston oikeustieteellisen tiedekunnan julkaisuja, Urheiluoikeuden sarja 1, Turku 2003).
123. *See also* Olli Rauste, *Urheiluoikeus*, 755–762 (Helsinki Lakimiesliiton Kustannus 1997).

3 of the Arbitration Act, an arbitration agreement must be in writing.[124] An arbitration agreement is in writing if it is contained in a document signed by the parties or in an exchange of letters between the parties. An arbitration agreement is also in writing when the parties, by exchanging telegrams or telexes or other such documents, have agreed that a dispute must be decided by one or more arbitrators. Additionally, an arbitration agreement is also in writing if an agreement, which has been made in the manner mentioned above, refers to a document containing an arbitration clause. In the context of sport, an interesting question concerns whether an arbitration clause in sports rules or regulations fulfils these criteria. It is stated in section 4 of the Arbitration Act that arbitration clauses in wills, deeds of gift, bills of lading, or similar documents in the by-laws of an association, a foundation, a limited liability company or of another company or corporate entity, and by which the parties or the person against whom a claim is made, must have the same effect as arbitration agreements.

266. A valid arbitration agreement precludes any opportunity to bring an action before a general court. A court before which an action is brought in a matter that is the subject of an arbitration agreement must, if a party so requests, and not later than when submitting the first statement on the substance of the dispute, refer the parties to arbitration. A decision given by one or more arbitrators is final. However, general courts are involved in the enforcement of arbitral awards. A decision on enforcement of an arbitral award must be made by a District Court.

267. An application for the enforcement of an arbitral award, submitted to the court in the first instance, must be accompanied by the original arbitration agreement or the provision referred to in section 4 of the Finnish Arbitration Act, and by the original arbitral award or certified copies thereof. A document drawn up in any other language than Finnish or Swedish must, furthermore, be accompanied by a certified translation into either of these languages, unless the court grants an exemption. Before an application is granted, the party against whom the enforcement is sought must be given an opportunity to be heard, unless there is a special reason to the contrary. Unless a witness or another person is to be heard in person, the District Court must deal with the matter in chambers.

268. The court may refuse an application, referred to in section 43 of the Finnish Arbitration Act, only if it finds that the award, on grounds referred to in section 40 of the Finnish Arbitration Act, is null and void or if the arbitral award has been set aside by a court, or if a court, because of an action declaring an award null and void or for setting it aside, has ordered that any enforcement of the award must be interrupted or suspended.

269. Arbitration governed by the Finnish Arbitration Act is, at least in some cases, a reliable way to acquire a final decision for sports-related disputes. Arbitration is not by definition public, and it is, in most cases, faster than a trial before a

124. *See*, e.g., Matti S. Kurkela, *Välimiesmenettelylaki*, 23–26 (Helsinki Lakimiesliiton Kustannus 1996).

general court. Additionally, parties can have an active role when appointing arbitrators, which can be important in cases dealing with sport and sporting activities. However, the costs of arbitration can be high and this has to be taken into consideration before signing an arbitration agreement. In practice, arbitration has had a significant role in disputes concerning player's agreement. In other contexts, arbitration has had only a limited position in the Finnish sporting system.[125]

III. The Finnish Sports Arbitration Board

A. Introduction

270. The Finnish Sports Arbitration Board was established in 1991 as an independent organ for dispute resolution in sport. The establishment of the Finnish Sports Arbitration Board can be seen as a part of the juridification process of sport in Finland in the 1990s. The Finnish Sports Arbitration Board was established by the central Finnish sports organizations, which found it necessary to have a separate organization that could consider and decide disputes concerning sport independently and competently. An independent organization would also diminish pressures to have sport-related disputes conducted before general courts or through arbitration. At the same time, the Anti-Doping Convention of the Council of Europe required clear and enforceable provisions for appealing against any judgment made in doping cases.[126]

271. The Finnish Sports Arbitration Board has gained a central position as an organization handling and solving disputes related to Finnish sport. Practically all sports federations in Finland have recognized the status and competence of the Finnish Sports Arbitration Board. An interesting question concerns the relationship between the Finnish sports leagues and the Finnish Sports Arbitration Board. All the major sports leagues have given their consent to the Finnish Sports Arbitration Board to deal with cases related to these leagues.

272. The legal status and competence of the Finnish Sports Arbitration Board is not based on legislation.[127] On the contrary, the competence of the Finnish Sports Arbitration Board to consider and decide cases is defined in its rules. A party or an appellant before the Finnish Sports Arbitration Board can be an athlete, another individual or a legal person whose rights are affected by the contested decision. The Finnish Sports Arbitration Board can investigate the decisions of an association concerning the expulsion of a member from an association, diminishing a member's

125. *See also* Heikki Halila, *Piirteitä lahden MM-hiihtojen dopingskandaalin oikeudellisista ulottuvuuksista*, Defensor Legis 823, 838–840 (2001).
126. Council of Europe, Anti-Doping Convention, Strasbourg 16.XI.1989, European Treaty Series – No. 135.
127. *See also* Pertti Välimäki, *Urheilun oikeusturvalautakunnan toimivallasta ja sen jäsenten asemasta*, Urheilu ja oikeus 211, 212–216 (2011).

rule-based rights in an association or disciplinary sanctions. Additionally, the Finnish Sports Arbitration Board can examine whether a decision was made which was against the rules of an association or sports rules and regulations. However, this competence does not cover the rules of a game.

273. The Finnish Sports Arbitration Board can also evaluate whether an athlete has been chosen to participate in the Olympic Games, World Championships, and other major international sports events according to the criteria set in advance by a sports federation; the evaluation can consider also whether the decision was discriminatory on the grounds of age, religion, opinion, origin or any other reason that concerns the athlete as a person.[128]

274. In doping cases, an athlete or other person can challenge a decision based on the Finnish Anti-Doping Code made by the FINCIS before the Finnish Sports Arbitration Board. The FINCIS can participate, as a party, in the process before the Finnish Sports Arbitration Board in these cases.

275. The Finnish Sports Arbitration Board cannot consider a case which is pending before a court of law or in arbitration. This limitation of competence is justified when taking into consideration the legal status of the Finnish Sports Arbitration Board. However, the Finnish Sports Arbitration Board can base its competence on the Finnish Arbitration Act when parties in a single case agree to do so. In practice, this opens up a valid route for athletes and sports organizations to have a clear and direct procedure for obtaining a final decision for their disputes. Sports organizations also have an option to ask for legal statements in cases which are not pending before the Finnish Sports Arbitration Board.

B. Composition of the Finnish Sports Arbitration Board and Appointment of Its Members

276. The Finnish Sports Arbitration Board has a chairperson, the necessary number of vice-chairpersons and at least seventeen members. The Board must have a quorum of a chairperson or vice-chairperson and a minimum of two members present when considering a case. In practice, there are chairperson or vice-chairperson and four members present. According to the rules of the Board, each party can choose one member of the quorum. This option has only been used on rare occasions.

277. When the competence of the Finnish Sports Arbitration Board is based on the Finnish Arbitration Act, the number of arbitrators must be three, unless otherwise agreed by the parties. Both parties can nominate one arbitrator. Otherwise, arbitrators are nominated by the chairperson of the Finnish Sports Arbitration Board. However, the chairperson of the Finnish Sports Arbitration Board or person nominated by him or her always functions as the chairperson of the arbitration

128. *See also* Heikki Halila, *Oikeudellistuva urheilu*, 460–465 (Helsinki Talentum 2006).

panel. In the cases of one arbitrator, he or she is nominated by the parties when a unanimous decision is reached. Otherwise, the arbitrator is nominated by the chairperson of the Finnish Sports Arbitration Board.

278. The Finnish Sports Arbitration Board has a fixed term of four calendar years.[129] The FOC invites the chairperson and vice-chairperson and nominates the members of the Finnish Sports Arbitration Board. All the above-mentioned members of the Finnish Sports Arbitration Board must have a legal education which, in practice, means a Master of Law degree. Additionally, the chairperson and vice-chairperson must have working experience as judges in a court of law.

279. Members of the Finnish Sports Arbitration Board are nominated among lawyers who have considerable expertise on the practical conditions of athletes and sports organizations. Before the nomination, the FOC must consult national athletes' organizations and other expert organizations. A lawyer who is approaching the age at which judges resign, according to the Finnish legal system, during the upcoming term cannot be nominated as a member of the Finnish Sports Arbitration Board.

280. The Finnish Sports Arbitration Board can nominate legal secretaries to work as referendaries. Legal secretaries prepare the cases for a main hearing or for a decision upon presentation. The division of work between legal secretaries is decided by the Finnish Sports Arbitration Board. In individual cases, the Finnish Sports Arbitration Board can even call an expert witness to be heard.

C. Procedure and Decision-Making in the Finnish Sports Arbitration Board

281. The Finnish Sports Arbitration Board deals with appeals against decisions made by sports federations, sports clubs, and other sports organizations. An appeal must only be considered when all the internal appeal procedures of a sports federation have been employed and the procedural requirements based on the rules of the Finnish Sports Arbitration Board are fulfilled.

282. The deadline date for the lodging of a written appeal is thirty days from the day when the decision was made available to the parties. A person who, due to a valid excuse, was unable to lodge an appeal, may, on an application, be granted a new deadline. If, due to a lawful excuse or another acceptable reason, an appeal cannot be sought in time, the Finnish Sports Arbitration Board must on request set a new appeal deadline. However, this deadline must not be later than one year after making the original decision.

283. The party must deliver the appeal document to the registry of the Finnish Sports Arbitration Board on the deadline date for the lodging of the appeal, at the

129. *See also* Heikki Halila, *Oikeudellistuva urheilu*, 89–91 (Helsinki Talentum 2006).

latest. The appeal document can also be delivered via post or e-mail. An appeal that is not presented on time must be dismissed without considering the merits.

284. The party must prove, when delivering the appeal document that he or she has paid the fee for the appeal. This fee is decided annually by the Finnish Sports Arbitration Board. Currently, the fee is EUR 800 for a legal person and EUR 300 for private persons. If a party wins his or her case before the Finnish Sports Arbitration Board, the fee will be returned. If a party partially wins his or her case before the Finnish Sports Arbitration Board, the fee or part of it can be returned.

285. The appeal document, which must be addressed to the Finnish Sports Arbitration Board, must indicate the decision that is being appealed and the reasons for the changes. The appeal document must be signed by the appellant or, if he or she has not drawn it up, by the person who has drawn up the appeal document. The decision that is being appealed or a copy of it must be attached to the appeal document. In doping cases, a written statement of the FINCIS must also be provided.

286. A member or a secretary of the Finnish Sports Arbitration Board is disqualified from acting in matters where the member or the secretary or his or her close relative is a party, and also when the member or the secretary or his or her close relative is to act or has acted as the representative, counsel or attorney of a party, or it can be anticipated that the decision in the matter will be to the specific advantage or disadvantage of the member or the secretary, or his or her close relative.[130] Additionally, a member or a secretary of the Finnish Sports Arbitration Board is disqualified in a matter if he or she is a member or a person elected to a position of trust of an association who is a party to or is in service with or in a pertinent commission relationship to the party. A member or a secretary of the Finnish Sports Arbitration Board must also be disqualified if his or her impartiality is compromised for any other special reason.

287. A party may retain the services of an attorney or a counsel before the Finnish Sports Arbitration Board.

288. Proceedings before the Board are not made public unless decided otherwise by the Finnish Sports Arbitration Board in a single case, with the consent of the parties. Trial documents before the Finnish Sports Arbitration Board are not public unless decided otherwise by the Finnish Sports Arbitration Board in a single case with the consent of the parties.

289. The Finnish Sports Arbitration Board must decide a case on the basis of the written trial material. An oral hearing is held if necessary for the sake of the clarity of a case. The Finnish Sports Arbitration Board must invite the parties to the oral

130. *See also* Pertti Välimäki, *Urheilun oikeusturvalautakunnan toimivallasta ja sen jäsenten asemasta*, Urheilu ja oikeus 211, 246–253 (2011).

hearing. Witnesses and expert witnesses can be heard in the oral hearing if the Finnish Sports Arbitration Board so order. Parties and members of the Finnish Sports Arbitration Board can propose that witnesses and expert witnesses are heard in the oral hearing.

290. Before the matter is decided, a party must be reserved an opportunity to express an opinion on the matter and submit an explanation on the other party's demands, and provide information which may have an effect on the decision of the Finnish Sports Arbitration Board. A matter must be considered without undue delay, mainly in one hearing.

291. In a vote, the opinion supported by the majority of the members prevails. In the event of a tie, the opinion more lenient to the defendant is to prevail in disciplinary cases and doping cases. Otherwise, the opinion supported by the chairperson must prevail. The decision of the Finnish Sports Arbitration Board must be accompanied with reasons. The Finnish Sports Arbitration Board sends copies of its decision to all parties and, in doping cases, to the sports association, which the party is representing, and to the FINCIS. The Finnish Sports Arbitration Board may send the decision by post or via e-mail.

292. A decision of the Finnish Sports Arbitration Board may not be appealed against unless otherwise stated in the Finnish Anti-Doping Code. By request of a party, the Finnish Sports Arbitration Board may reconsider a case under conditions where reference is made to a circumstance or piece of evidence that has not been presented earlier, and its presentation would probably have led to a different result. Reconsideration is also possible, by request of a party, if the relevant case law in Finland or elsewhere has considerably changed. Reconsideration must not lead to a more severe sanction in disciplinary cases and doping cases. Reconsideration must be requested within five years of the original decision of the Finnish Sports Arbitration Board.

293. The decision of the Finnish Sports Arbitration Board is made public. However, the Finnish Sports Arbitration Board may order that the reasons for the decision be kept secret to a certain extent. Nevertheless, a party has the right to be informed about the reasons. The publicity of an arbitral award given by the Finnish Sports Arbitration Board is decided based on the Finnish Arbitration Act. There are also different norms concerning the publicity of decisions given in doping cases. The decisions of the Finnish Sports Arbitration Board are published on its webpage. Based on the discretion of the Finnish Sports Arbitration Board, various parts of a decision may be left unpublished if they involve particularly sensitive aspects of the private life of a party.

294. A member or a secretary of the Finnish Sports Arbitration Board must not express or use any information about a party which he or she has acquired when considering a case before the Finnish Sports Arbitration Board if this information must, based on its nature, be kept secret unless consent is given by this party. The deliberations and votes of the Finnish Sports Arbitration Board must be held without the presence of the parties and the public. The contents of the deliberations must be kept secret.

295. The party who loses the case is liable for all or part of the reasonable legal costs incurred by the opposing party, based on the discretion of the Finnish Sports Arbitration Board. In exceptional circumstances, the Finnish Sports Arbitration Board can declare that there is reason to order that the parties are to be liable for their own legal costs, even if one party has lost his or her case. If the party claiming legal costs has only partially won his or her case, the Finnish Sports Arbitration Board must consider how the legal costs are divided between the parties or declare that the parties are liable for their own legal costs. The Finnish Sports Arbitration Board can, when dismissing a case, state that the legal issues in the case have been so unclear that the losing party has had a justifiable reason to pursue the proceedings and order that the parties are to be liable for their own legal costs. When the Finnish Arbitration Board functions as an arbitration panel, claims concerning legal costs are decided based on the Finnish Arbitration Act.

Part II. Sport and Employment

Chapter 1. Legal Background

296. There are various relevant aspects when evaluating an athlete's legal position in sport. Some of these perspectives have been chosen here for further evaluation. It is justified to assume that questions concerning the legal basis for earning a livelihood are of the utmost importance for athletes. In practice, the relevant questions concern the conditions under which an employment contract has been drafted between an athlete and a sports club or other actors in sport.[131] This question is highly important, at least, for players in team sports. Their legal position has to be evaluated based on the Finnish Employment Contracts Act (55/2001).

297. In Finland, there is no legislation especially applicable to employment relationships or employment contracts in sport. Therefore, all the relevant questions are evaluated based on general labour law. The Employment Contracts Act (55/2001) applies to contracts (employment contracts) entered into by an employee, or jointly by several employees as a team, agreeing personally to perform work for an employer under the employer's direction and supervision in return for payment or some other remuneration. The Act applies regardless of the absence of any agreement on remuneration if the facts indicate that the work was not intended to be performed without remuneration. Application of the Act is not prevented merely by the fact that the work is performed at the employee's home or in a place chosen by the employee, or by the fact that the work is performed using the employee's implements or machinery.

298. In the legal literature, the criteria for an employment relationship have been clearly defined (the performance of work; contract, the work is performed for the other party; remuneration; and direction and supervision).[132] First, the concept of work is wide. Basically, all kinds of work may be the subject of a contract of employment. Second, the work mentioned in section 1 of the Employment Contracts Act has to be performed on a contractual basis in order to fall within the scope

131. *See* generally Esa Schön, *Pelaajasopimus. Tutkimus joukkueurheilijoiden pelaajasopimusten tyypillisestä sisällöstä, erityispiirteistä ja oikeusvaikutuksista*, 31–34 (Helsinki Unigrafia 2021), and Perttu Turku, *Yksilöurheilijan työoikeudellinen asema talliurheilussa*, 5–12 (Turun yliopiston oikeustieteellisen tiedekunnan julkaisuja, Urheiluoikeuden sarja 2, Turku 2003).

132. *See*, e.g., Arvo Sipilä, *Suomen työoikeuden käsite ja järjestelmä sekä suhde sosiaaliseen lainsäädäntöön* (Helsinki 1938).

of the employment relationship. In principle, the formation of an employment contract requires consistent declarations of intent from both of the contracting parties although, according to section 3 of the Employment Contracts Act, an employment contract may be oral, written, or in an electronic form. Third, the criterion for performing work for the other party requires that there is a legal relationship between the two parties. Fourth, the work has to be performed in return for payment or some other remuneration. Fifth, the work has to be performed under the direction and supervision of the employer. All of these criteria need to be fulfilled in order to have an employment relationship in a concrete case. In practice, an overall assessment is needed when deciding whether the Employment Contracts Act is applicable or not.

299. Initially, it was an open question whether athletes in team sports could be qualified as employees or not. Among the professionalization of Finnish team sports, the legal position of players in team sports has developed gradually in case law. The Supreme Court gave some important precedents in the 1990s, which clarified the team player's legal position.

300. In the first case, the decision of the Supreme Court concerned an American basketball player who had signed a written player agreement with a Finnish basketball club in exchange for USD 42,500, housing, and a car benefit.[133] The player agreement contained a 'no cut clause' according to which the club had no right to cancel the agreement after a specified date. Despite the above-mentioned clause, the club cancelled the contract after this date on the basis of a continuous breach of contract. The player considered that there was an employment contract between the parties and claimed damages by referring to the 'no cut clause'. The Supreme Court stated that the club had justified grounds based on the Employment Contracts Act to cancel the employment contract. It is significant from the legal perspective that the Supreme Court evaluated for the first time a player agreement in the context of the Employment Contracts Act. This can be seen as the beginning of a new era in sport and sports law in Finland.

301. The second relevant decision of the Supreme Court also concerned an American basketball player who had signed a written contract with a Finnish basketball team.[134] Unfortunately, the player agreement was never signed by the club. The player was for a short time in the service of the above-mentioned club, but soon after his arrival, the player signed another player contract with another basketball club. The first club sued the player and the second club for the breach of a player agreement and claimed damages. The player and the second club claimed that there was no contract between the player and the first club. Additionally, they claimed that it was a contract of employment with a probation time, during which the employment contract may be cancelled by either party.

---

133. KKO 1993:40.
134. KKO 1993:43.

302. The Supreme Court stated that the player had, in principle, a right to cancel the employment contract. However, the mere fact that the player was offered a contract with a higher salary by another club was an inappropriate cause for the cancellation of the player agreement and contrary to the Employment Contracts Act. The significance of this decision lies in the fact that the Supreme Court explicitly discussed in its ruling whether a professional athlete could fulfil the criteria for an employee defined in the Employment Contracts Act. The answer was definitively affirmative.

303. The third case considered by the Supreme Court concerned a Finnish ice hockey player who had signed a player agreement with a first-division team.[135] According to the player agreement, the player was to receive a monthly salary of EUR 706 amounting to a total of EUR 4,236 for the season. It transpired, however, that the team was not a registered association governed by the Finnish Association Act (503/1999). The liability for an obligation caused by an act on behalf of an unregistered association rests with the persons who took part in the act or decided on it personally, jointly, or severally. Therefore, the Supreme Court held the two people, who acted on behalf of the unregistered association, personally liable for the commitment. The most important part is that the Supreme Court stated that the player agreement fulfilled the criteria set in section 1 of the Employment Contracts Act and was qualified as an employment contract. The decision was in line with the previously discussed decision KKO 1993:42.

304. The fourth case before the Supreme Court defined the relationship between an employment relationship and a hobby.[136] The player brought an action before a district court and asked for a declaratory judgment against the State of Finland. The district court was asked to declare that the written player agreement concluded between the player and an ice hockey club should be evaluated within the context of the Employment Contracts Act. Based on the player agreement, the player was obliged to practice and play ice hockey in the team according to the instructions of the management of the club. Additionally, the player was entitled to have point money payments for regular season games, a bonus payment if the team qualified for the Finnish national league, and some compensation for travel expenses. It was stipulated by the parties that the player agreement was not regarded as an employment contract.

305. The Supreme Court stated that it was not required in section 1 of the Employment Contracts Act that a payment should exceed a certain amount in order to qualify as genuine remuneration. The Supreme Court stated further that the remuneration cannot be so small that it is only symbolic. According to the player agreement, the player could expect to receive fees which were not only ostensible. During the season in question, the player had received fees and compensations amounting to over EUR 2,000. In these circumstances, the remuneration must be considered as

135. KKO 1995:45.
136. KKO 1997:38.

remuneration for work and not a subsidy given to support a leisure time activity. The Supreme Court stated that the Employment Contracts Act was applicable in the case.

306. The above-mentioned decision was not a surprise when taking into consideration the previous case law. It seems that, based on this case law, the legal position of players in team sports is firmly defined. In principle, players are regarded as employees when they receive remuneration payments and compensations that are not merely symbolic.[137] This legal background has to be taken into consideration when preparing player agreements in sport. Simultaneously, players and sports clubs have to recognize all the duties and rights which are the result of the Employment Contracts Act being applied in an individual contractual relationship. Basically, it is a question of contractual governance and risk management which form a central part of the relevant expertise nowadays required in sport.

307. There are various sections in the Employment Contracts Act which are highly relevant to sport. If the requirements of these sections are not duly investigated in sport, major legal challenges might occur. A typical feature of player agreements is that they are made for a specific fixed term.[138] According to section 3 of the Employment Contracts Act, justified reasons are required for signing a fixed-term employment contract. It is the duty of both parties to present these reasons in a single case and write them into an employment contract.

308. Sometimes trial periods are used in sport. According to the Employment Contracts Act, the employer and the employee may agree on a trial period of a maximum of four months starting from the beginning of the work. During the trial period, the employment contract may be cancelled by either party. The employment contract may not, however, be cancelled on grounds which are otherwise inappropriate with regard to the purpose of the trial period.

309. General obligations for both the employer and the employee are defined in the Employment Contracts Act. They form a solid basis for each employment relationship. The employer must in all respects work to improve employer-employee relations and relations among the employees. The employer should ensure that employees are able to carry out their work even when the enterprise's operations, the work to be carried out or the work methods are changed or developed. The employer should strive to further the employees' opportunities to develop themselves according to their abilities so that they can advance in their careers.

137. *See also* Henri Helo, *Työehtosopimukset urheilussa*, 5–8 (Opetusministeriö, Kulttuuripolitiikan osaston julkaisusarja 4/2000, Helsinki 2000).

138. *See also* Esa Schön, *Pelaajasopimus. Tutkimus joukkueurheilijoiden pelaajasopimusten tyypillisestä sisällöstä, erityispiirteistä ja oikeusvaikutuksista*, 34–39 and 112–126 (Helsinki Unigrafia 2021), and Esa Schön, *Joukkueurheilijan pelaajasopimus velvoiteoikeudellisena sopimustyyppinä*, 88–101 (Turun yliopiston oikeustieteellisen tiedekunnan julkaisuja, Urheiluoikeuden sarja 25, Turku 2010).

310. According to the Employment Contracts Act, employees should perform their work carefully, observing the instructions concerning performance issued by the employer within their competence. In their activities, employees should avoid everything that conflicts with the actions reasonably required of employees in their position. This concerns also competing activities. Employees should not do work for another party or engage in such activity that would, taking the nature of the work and the individual employee's position into account, cause or manifest harm to their employer as a competing activity, contrary to fair employment practices.

311. The terms of a player agreement might be breached or even the Employment Contracts Act may be violated by either party in individual cases. Chapter 12 of the Employment Contracts Act concerns liability for damages.[139] If the employer intentionally or through negligence commits a breach against obligations arising from the employment relationship or the Employment Contracts Act, it will be liable for the loss thus caused to the employee. If the employee intentionally or through negligence commits a breach against, or neglects obligations arising from, the employment contract or the Employment Contracts Act or at work causes a loss to the employer, the employee will be liable to the employer for the loss thus caused in accordance with the grounds laid down in Chapter 4, section 1, of the Tort Liability Act (412/1974).

312. In professional team sport, there is, at least in most cases, an employment contract between an athlete and a sports club. In this context, it is worth evaluating what is the competence of an employer to impose disciplinary sanctions on athletes. In most cases, an employer has no internal rules mentioned in the Finnish Association Act which can form the legal basis for disciplinary proceedings. The only exceptions concern national teams. An employer needs a legal basis for conducting disciplinary proceedings.

313. Sports clubs, as employers, have options other than disciplinary-related means to impose sanctions on athletes. These sanctions have a contractual basis and they can be used simultaneously with disciplinary sanctions imposed by a sports federation. In practice, it is typically a question of a partial deduction from an athlete's pay during a specified suspension period. However, it has to be remembered that an athlete's need to practice during the above-mentioned period has to be taken into consideration when making the decision.

314. Additionally, an athlete is liable for the compensation of damages which he has caused to the employer. According to Chapter 12, section 2 of the Employment Contracts Act (55/2001), if the employee intentionally or through negligence commits a breach against, or neglects obligations arising from, the employment contract or the Employment Contracts Act or at work causes a loss to the employer, the employee shall be liable to the employer for the loss thus caused in accordance with

139. *See also* Esa Schön, *Joukkueurheilijan pelaajasopimus velvoiteoikeudellisena sopimustyyppinä*, 143–148 (Turun yliopiston oikeustieteellisen tiedekunnan julkaisuja, Urheiluoikeuden sarja 25, Turku 2010).

the grounds laid down in Chapter 4, section 1 of the Tort Liability Act (412/1974).[140] This section can also be applied in disciplinary cases. In practice, there are often provisions concerning these situations in collective labour agreements between sports federations and players' federations.

315. In the legal context, the legal position of an employer can be evaluated in disciplinary proceedings. An employer and a sports federation can have divergent interests concerning disciplinary proceedings. It is not the fundamental task of disciplinary panels to ensure that the personal objectives of an employer are achieved in an individual case as this can lead to conflicts and challenging of the legal status of the proceedings. The same legal requirements for discipline proceedings are also relevant concerning individual athletes. An employer has to commit himself to following and respecting sports regulations and the disciplinary code of a sports federation or a league. In most cases, this is done by a contractual arrangement between an employer and a sports league. These contractual arrangements are de facto preconditions for participating in a league or other sports competition.

316. The Employment Contracts Act and the player agreement form the basic structure under which an employment relationship between a player and a sports club is evaluated. Additionally, there are some collective agreements between federations representing both athletes and sports clubs in Finland governing the terms for individual player agreements.[141] Ice hockey forms a good example of this governance structure in Finland. It is interesting to investigate how this structure is actually working and how it affects the terms for individual player agreements. At the same time, it is possible to discover how a player's position, based on the Employment Contracts Act, is reshaped to a certain extent by various contractual arrangements.

140. Heikki Halila, *Oikeudellistuva urheilu*, 372 (Helsinki Talentum 2006).

141. *See* generally Tuukka Pulkkinen, *Työehtosopimus jalkapalloliigaan – erityisesti sitovuussuhteista*, 57–58 (Turun yliopiston oikeustieteellisen tiedekunnan julkaisuja, Urheiluoikeuden sarja 12, Turku 2006).

Chapter 2. General Agreements

317. The Finnish Ice Hockey Players' Association (FHPA) is an interest group of ice hockey players in Finland.[142] The FHPA was founded in 1973. Its objective is to promote and supervise the players' status as employees by collective safeguarding of the players' interests. It also aims at taking care of the players' insurance and social security, as well as their educational opportunities beyond ice hockey. In order to achieve these goals, the Ice Hockey Players' Educational and Career Advancement Foundation was founded in 1982 and operates under the auspices of the FHPA. Additionally, the SJL, the Finnish Hockey League Ltd (SM League), and the FHPA have, together with the registered ice hockey agents, signed an agreement on the registration system of the agents pursuing agent activities in ice hockey. The purpose of the registration system is to provide the players and teams with information on agents acting in ice hockey, to keep records of the agents, and to promote the professional skills of the agents recorded in the register.

318. The FHPA signed, on 13 April 2021, the current general agreement with the SM League which is in charge of the organization of the ice hockey competitions at the top league level in Finland. The general agreement will be effective for four years (seasons 2020–2024). The general agreement is not a collective agreement defined by the Employment Contracts Act. However, the parties will continue to analyse individual issues and perspectives that should be included in the collective bargaining agreement and also consider the effect of the agreement on professional ice hockey and sports in Finland.

319. There are various dimensions to the general agreement. The parties have negotiated a model player contract to be used between the employers and the players, as well as possible amendments to be made to the contract during the term of the contract. The parties have agreed on how the Working Hours Act (605/1996) is to be applied in professional ice hockey in Finland. According to the general agreement, the players' and the employers' contracts are not subject to the provisions of the Working Hours Act on overtime or Sunday work, nor those concerning weekly free time.[143] This clause is based on the view of the nature of the players' work and the compensation structure. The players must have at least one day off per working week. As a rule, the aim is to arrange a day off for each week. However, if the series schedule or another reason so requires, the team can arrange these days off in another manner.

320. Arrangements concerning pensions and casualty insurance form an important part of the general agreement. The SM League negotiates the insurance conditions in compliance with the Act on Athletes' Accident and Pension Cover (276/2009) with an insurance company of its choice. The SM League submits the conditions of the insurance contract to the Players' Association. Each ice hockey

142. www.sjry.fi (accessed 5 Oct. 2015).

143. *See* generally Esa Palenius, *Työaikalain vaikutuksista joukkueurheiluun*, 1–3 (Opetusministeriö, Kulttuuripolitiikan osaston julkaisusarja 1/1998, Helsinki 1998).

club as an employer is obliged to take out insurance for every player in the SM League with whom it has signed a player contract. The employer must also take out insurance for players with a try out contract.

321. The player's share of the pension insurance premiums is agreed on the general agreement. According to the Act on Athletes' Accident and Pension Cover (276/2009), the share of pension insurance premiums of the insurance is 4.5% of the player's salary and compensations during the season. The players pay 2% of the share of the pension insurance premiums. These payments are withdrawn from the player's salary up to a maximum of EUR 130.720 (season 2023–2024). The amount is adjusted every year by using the wage coefficient specified in section 96 of the Employees Pensions Act (395/2006). The withdrawal has to cover the entire season, complying with the amount determined by the wage coefficient valid in the calendar year of the season start.

322. The employer, who pays the insurance premium to the insurance company, has the right to withdraw the player's share of the insurance premium from the salary and to pay it to the insurance company. The SM League supervises the obligation to insure in accordance with the law. The SM League has the right to require information from the employer concerning the organization of insurance protection. The SM League notifies the Players' Association of the employers' significant payment failures related to the insurance premiums. The parties have to negotiate the necessary measures in such cases.

323. Organization of the player's holidays is agreed in the general agreement. The ice hockey club as the employer has to grant the players of the SM League a training leave of a minimum of twenty-four working days (Monday to Saturday) which means four weeks consecutively after the last official game (regular season, play-off, or national team). The employer must also grant the players a training leave for the working days of the incomplete calendar week during which the players play their last official game in the series.

324. According to the general agreement, the employer has to organize the team's training sessions in such a manner that the training decided by the employer falls mainly on working days (Monday to Friday); this stipulation also includes any other joint events of the team that takes place more than two weeks before the first official match in the regular season. This restriction does not concern the exhibition games played during the collective training period. Additionally, the employer must grant the players of the SM League a holiday of thirty-six consecutive working days, which means a minimum of six weeks in the period between 1 June and 31 August.

325. For the players who have not turned 24 by the end of the holiday credit year or who have not played the minimum of 300 games in the SM League (or respective series), the holiday lasts at least twenty-four working days, i.e., four weeks. Players taking a period of independent training are entitled to use training sites or facilities targeted at players participating in joint training by the employer. During this time, the player has to train independently but according to the training programmes planned jointly by the team's principal coaches and the player.

326. The general agreement also concerns breakdowns of wage payments. The player and the ice hockey club as the employer can agree mutually, in a separate wage attachment, to divide the payment of wages over a period shorter than twelve months. If the employer and the player have agreed on other summer leave (independent summer training) in addition to this agreement, the payment of the wages for that period will be transferred so as to take place between 1 August and 30 April, as separately agreed between the employer and the player.

327. According to the general agreement, the employer should not make a player play more than eight exhibition games before the regular season. Possible Champions Hockey League (CHL) series games are regarded as exhibition games in this case. Tournament games consisting of two periods at the maximum (forty minutes of effective playtime) are counted as half a game in this respect. All games longer than that are counted as entire games. However, the employer can make the players who have not turned 24 by the end of the holiday credit year or have not played at least 150 games in the SM League play a maximum of ten exhibition games before the beginning of the regular season.

328. Health care forms a core area of the general agreement. The employer has to provide the players, at the employer's expense, with health care services to prevent and treat health problems caused by and directly related to playing. The employer has to cover the expenses of the medical examinations prescribed by the employer's physician. The employer has to arrange, at the employer's expense, a physical examination for the player fulfilling the jointly approved criteria (separate instructions have been issued on the contents of the physical examination). The employer also has to provide the players with regular muscular treatment and, if necessary, a chance to receive physical treatment on the doctor's orders. Before the player contract is signed, the player must undergo a physical examination in which a physician appointed by the employer examines and verifies his state of health and ability to play. The employer has to cover the expenses of this physical examination.

329. Professional ice hockey has a large commercial potential in Finland. Therefore, the transfer of intellectual property rights is a key factor for the realization of different campaigns and other events. The employer may use the players' photos (in the team uniform) and other identification data for marketing their own or their stakeholders' organizations, in any form of printed or electronic communication. The SM League may use the players' photos (in the team uniform) and other identification data for promoting its own or its stakeholders' organizations, in any form of printed or electronic communication. The FHPA can run its own commercial and other campaigns. Players may take part in the events and regular advertisement campaigns of the Players' Association under certain conditions. According to the general agreement, either the SM League or the FHPA is entitled to organize an 'All

Stars' or corresponding match every year. The organizer then has to return 30% of the match proceeds to the other contracting party.

330. There should be life after a professional ice hockey career. Therefore, the parties of the general agreement have agreed to work in cooperation to develop measures to promote the players' professional education during their ice hockey career and after it. The SM League and its member corporations contribute, for their part, to the creation of educational opportunities for the players and the combining of studies with the match and training programme.

331. The general agreement between the FHPA and the SM League is a distinguished example of a contractual arrangement defining players' rights and obligations on a collective level, although it does not have the legal status of a generally applicable collective agreement as mentioned in the Employments Contracts Act (55/2001). In practice, all the central issues, and most of the relevant details concerning professional ice hockey players' rights and obligations, are defined in the general agreement. This is not the case in every sport in Finland, but it seems to be the most potential direction for future development in other sports as well. Basically, this development is closely linked to the de facto status which players' and other athletes' organizations will have in the future. The stronger the position of these organizations becomes in the Finnish sports system, the greater their influence will be when negotiating player agreements and other contracts in the future.

Chapter 3. Player Agreements

332. The FHPA and the SM League, on 13 April 2021, agreed on the current general agreement and standard player contract form to be used for players in the Finnish Hockey League. The players' contract has close connections to the general agreement between the FHPA and the SM League, as discussed previously. These two contracts should be evaluated from a legal perspective in a comprehensive way.[144] In fact, a player contract signed by a player and an ice hockey club enforces at an individual level many issues decided by the FHPA and the Finnish Hockey League on a collective level. The nexus between these agreements is highly relevant when applying a player agreement in a concrete case.

333. The player agreement is agreed to be a fixed-term contract, which means that it is terminated without giving notice at the end of the fixed period.[145] If agreed, the employer and the player can give notice to terminate the contract for the defined season by a specified date. The notice must be given in writing. There is a trial period in the player agreement. During the trial period, the player's contract can be cancelled by each party. The trial period can last for a maximum of four months. In a player contract shorter than eight months, the trial period can cover a maximum of half of the term of the contract. The trial period should not exceed the date of 31 December. The player contract enters into force after the employer has received a medical report or after the parties have agreed that a physical examination is not necessary.

334. There are some general provisions defined in the player agreement. Each player has to agree to play and practice with the Finnish team which belongs to the organization and to which he is appointed by the employer, in accordance with the employer's and the coaching staff's orders. The employer and the player can mutually agree in advance that the player will be transferred to another employer's team.

335. Disciplinary rules must have a valid legal basis that is legally constructed by the player agreement. Players must commit to complying, as part of this contract, with the disciplinary rules of the Finnish Hockey League and the SJL and the IIHF, as well as the Finnish Anti-Doping Code. This means accepting the fact that the SM League, or a body or person appointed by the SM League can impose sanctions on the player in accordance with the said regulations. Additionally, the player accepts the fact that the employer and the SM League can keep a public register of the penalties imposed as a disciplinary measure. The official approved disciplinary rules, which the SM League submits to the Finnish Hockey Players' Association before their entry into force, should be attached to the player contract.

144. *See also* Heikki Halila, *Urheilusopimukset*, 282–285 (in Heikki Halila & Mika Hemmo (eds), Sopimustyypit (2nd ed., Helsinki Talentum 2008)).

145. *See also* Esa Schön, *Joukkueurheilijan pelaajasopimus velvoiteoikeudellisena sopimustyyppinä*, 88–101 (Turun yliopiston oikeustieteellisen tiedekunnan julkaisuja, Urheiluoikeuden sarja 25, Turku 2010).

336. Disciplinary rules can be enforced in many ways; one of them is defined in the player agreement. The employer is entitled to withdraw an amount corresponding to X/180 of the player's season-specific wages if the player is sentenced to a penalty in two games or more (X = length of the penalty).[146] If the player is sentenced to another penalty in two games or more during the same season, the employer is entitled to withdraw an amount corresponding to X/120 of the player's salary. If the player is sentenced to a third or subsequent penalty in two games or more during the same season, the employer is entitled to withdraw an amount corresponding to X/60 of the player's salary. Withdrawals from the player's salary are paid to the SM League who then allocates the funds thus accumulated to support the operations of the SM League Alumni and to hire a study counsellor for the League. While making the deduction from the player's salary, the employer should pay attention to the restrictions specified in section 2:17 of the Employment Contracts Act (55/2001).

337. Anti-doping programmes form an important part of professional sport. Therefore, it is evident that anti-doping rules and regulations should be mentioned in the player agreement. It is also necessary to have a valid legal basis for anti-doping procedures and sanctions. According to the player agreement, players are liable to comply with the Finnish Anti-Doping Code and, in accordance with it, participate in tests ordained by the employer, the SM League, the SJL, the FINCIS, or another body binding upon the SM League or the SJL. These tests are necessary in order to find out if the player has been using forbidden substances while performing sports. The player must also take a drug test on the employer's demand.

338. Doping cases have various dimensions. Some cases also concern the contractual relationship between a player and a sports club. According to the player contract, if the player is found guilty of using substances that are prohibited in sports or of another infringement according to the Finnish Anti-doping Code, the employer may discontinue paying the compensations laid down in the contract with immediate effect. If the player is sentenced to a suspension for violating the anti-doping regulations, the employer may terminate the contract with immediate effect, in which case the player is liable to remunerate the club for the damage he has caused. The indemnification is determined, unless it can be agreed upon, through the arbitration proceedings specified in the player contract.

339. Various duties of the players are defined in the player agreement. The player agrees to participate in the regular advertising and promotional events determined by the employer, as well as in events arranged in cooperation with the employer's partners. The player has to comply with the employer's advertising, marketing and cooperation agreements if the employer and the player have agreed to this in the player agreement. The employer has to provide an account of these agreements on request. The player must not fail to comply with the employer's

146. *See* generally Esa Schön, *Joukkueurheilijan pelaajasopimus velvoiteoikeudellisena sopimustyyppinä*, 145–148 (Turun yliopiston oikeustieteellisen tiedekunnan julkaisuja, Urheiluoikeuden sarja 25, Turku 2010).

advertising, marketing and cooperation agreements, nor should he sign such agreements without the employer's permission. When refusing to grant permission, the employer must present well-founded reasons for the refusal that are directly connected with the employer's operations.

340. Intellectual property rights are essential when making commercial agreement, for example, sponsorship agreements, in sport. Therefore, it is evident that conditions for the transfer of intellectual property rights are defined in the player agreement. According to the player agreement, the employer holds the exclusive right to use photographs of the player in the team uniform or other respective means of identification. The employer can use such photographs for marketing their own or their stakeholders' organizations, in any printed or electronic form of communication. The player can use his own photo in the team uniform if the employer grants him specific permission to do so. The player should use a hockey stick and other equipment of the trademark determined by the employer unless agreed otherwise. The player should use the equipment determined by the employer in the games, training sessions, and other events of the employer.

341. There are some clauses in the player agreement which directly concern ice hockey operations in the clubs. According to the player agreement, if a player is inhibited from taking part in the team's training sessions or games due to a force majeure, he must let the team's coaching staff know about the inhibition and its grounds without delay. Players must maintain their physical condition through independent training during the period when the team does not have organized joint training sessions. Players should take part in physical fitness tests as ordained by the coaching staff. Such physical fitness tests have to be arranged at times that do not overlap with the team's general holidays.

342. The player agreement does not only govern how players should behave when working but also players' activities in their leisure time. Players should not perform sports detrimental to the player's health (e.g., motor sports, sky diving) unless accepted by the club in an individual player agreement. However, players are allowed to participate in other sports in a normal manner if they support or improve the player's basic physical condition and performance in ice hockey. The player agreement also concerns players' public appearances. Players should work to promote the positive image of their team and ice hockey in all aspects of their public appearances, and to refrain from everything that might be in conflict with these aims. Players should lead their private life in a way that does not endanger their ability and capacity to play or inflict negative publicity on the team or ice hockey in general.

343. Match-fixing is one of the major problems in sport.[147] All necessary actions should be taken in order to prevent match-fixing and other illegal acts concerning betting. Therefore, it is logical that there are terms concerning betting in the player

147. *See also* Niko Matikainen, *Sopupelit, fair play ja vedonlyntipetos*, 6–12 (Turun yliopiston oikeustieteellisen tiedekunnan julkaisuja, Urheiluoikeuden sarja 11, Turku 2006).

agreement. By signing the player agreement, players agree not to participate in gambling or betting on their own team's games themselves or by asking another person to represent them. Nor should they act in a manner that might call into question their actions or their employer's position towards gambling or pool games.

344. The player agreement is not one-sided in favour of the employers, although the players' duties are widely defined. There are also some terms concerning employers' duties in the player agreement. Payment of wages is the main obligation for employers. According to the player agreement, the employer has to pay the salary, compensations, and other remunerations to a player, as agreed in the player compensation agreement attached to the contract. Based on Finnish legislation, part of the salary can be transferred to the Athletes' Fund. Therefore, the employer should pay, on the player's request, a part of the salary determined by the player to the Athletes' Fund, as defined in section 16 a–c of the Income Tax Act (1535/1992).

345. Ice hockey is a dangerous sport and players should be properly insured. The employer must take out insurance for the player in accordance with the Act on Athletes' Accident and Pension Cover (276/2009). The employer should also take into account the specifications concerning the contents of the insurance cover laid down in the general agreement and the protocol between the SM League and the FHPA. The employer is responsible for paying the insurance premium to the insurance company. On the basis of the player contract, the player accepts that the employer withholds 0%–2% points of his wages (up to a maximum of EUR 130.720) as a pension insurance premium and pays it to the insurance company. A player can improve his insurance cover at his own expense. Such voluntary insurance will not affect the employer's liability to insure the player in accordance with the player agreement. Players also accept that the employer will inform the SM League of any issues relevant to the monitoring of the insurance cover.

346. In cases of illness or injury, when a player is not able to fulfil his obligations based on the player agreement, there are terms concerning the procedures and material issues for this in the player agreement. First, a player has to notify the team's coaching staff without delay if he falls ill or is injured. Second, illness or injury can affect the employer's duty to pay the agreed compensation and various situations can occur in this respect.

347. According to the player agreement, if a player is injured or falls ill in one of the team's games or training sessions, on a trip to a game or training session, or in a social event in which he takes part following the team's orders or while he is practising to keep up his physical condition independently and a physician appointed by the team finds the player unable to play, then the employer has to pay the compensation agreed in full until the end of the ongoing season. In addition, if a multi-year contract is valid, the employer has to pay the compensation in full from the beginning of the season following the injury (1 May) for six months.[148] If the

148. However, for September and October, 50% of the wages will be paid for the part of the monthly dividend of the annual wages exceeding EUR 130.700.

player falls ill or is injured for a reason other than the one mentioned above, the employer has to pay the player the compensation specified in the player agreement during the validity of the player contract, as of the beginning of the period of incapacity to play.[149] The player must present a reliable report to the employer concerning his or her incapacity to play. However, a player is not entitled to salary during the period of his incapacity to work if he has caused the incapacity wilfully or by gross negligence. Additionally, the employer may deduct per diems and other corresponding compensations, which the player receives by virtue of the law or following an agreement with the employer, from the player's salary during the period of his incapacity to work.

348. Some terms concerning breaches and dissolution are established in the player agreement. The employer and the player are entitled to dissolve the contract irrespective of its duration with immediate effect if there are particularly weighty reasons. Such reasons include a breach or negligence of the legal or contractual obligations involved in the employment relationship that are so serious that the other party cannot be reasonably expected to continue the contractual relationship. If either of the contracting parties has misled the other contracting party with respect to essential provisions of the contract, the misled party has the right to dissolve the contract with immediate effect and to be remunerated for the damage incurred. Any dispute or controversy arising from a player's contract should be resolved through arbitration proceedings, in compliance with the effective legislation on arbitration proceedings.[150]

349. The current player agreement is the result of a long negotiation process and the culture of the FHPA and the SM League. Presumably, some difficulties concerning standard player contracts might be circumvented because the above-mentioned parties seem to have an equal position in the negotiations. In these circumstances, a balance of interest can be achieved. In the long-term, this is an appropriate state of affairs for both parties. Even in sport, contractual stability is a precondition for success and efficient end-results.

350. The relevant context has to be taken into consideration when preparing a player contract in every sport. This context also affects the decisions on individual terms of the player agreement. Therefore, direct solutions to problems in other sports cannot be found in the above-mentioned player agreement. However, the basic principles and the general structure of the player agreement are also valuable in other sports. Evidently, these guidelines have been followed and will be followed in other sports in Finland when preparing new models and structures for player agreements.

149. These compensations concern salaries for the maximum of two months, if the player contract was signed after 31 October during the ongoing season, and salaries for the maximum of five months, if the player contract was signed by 31 October during the ongoing season.
150. The Finnish Arbitration Act (967/1992).

Part III. Doping and Sport

Chapter 1. General Issues

351. Rivalry between athletes, teams, and nations has always been a central feature in sport. This rivalry is, at the same time, a factor which holds different aspects of sport together and provides an impulse for the development of sport. The desire to win and achieve success has had many consequences in sport. One of these is the constant need to update the borderline between what is allowed and what is prohibited in sport. In order to win matches and competitions, some athletes and teams have been prepared to circumvent sport rules and regulations or, at least, to interpret them in a way that is most favourable for themselves. In addition, athletes have also tried to enhance their sport's performance artificially.

352. Doping is not a new phenomenon although the commercialization of sport has increased its importance during the last decades. Doping can be a problem even in recreational sport but, in most cases, the greatest problems concern professional and competitive sport because there are enormous economic aspects in these fields of sport.[151] Therefore, the legal status of a lifetime ineligibility sanction based on anti-doping rules is evaluated in these contexts.

353. It is typical for sport that violations of sports regulations and also anti-doping codes are sanctioned in internal procedures. Following a violation, a discipline proceeding can be opened. In the legal context, it is essential that these proceedings have a solid legal basis.[152] Therefore, it has to be evaluated how athletes, coaches, and other officials are bound by discipline rules and proceedings.

354. Different sanctions can be imposed in disciplinary proceedings. Some of these sanctions can be severe. An example of these severe sanctions that can be mentioned is the lifetime ineligibility sanction which can be issued for certain anti-doping rule violations. There are many interesting legal aspects concerning this

151. *See also* Sami Teräväinen, *Kurinpito ja kontrolli huippu-urheilun dopingasiassa. Esimerkkinä Tour de Francen ja ammattipyöräilyn dopingtapaukset*, 17–31 (Turun yliopiston oikeustieteellisen tiedekunnan julkaisuja, Urheiluoikeuden sarja 27, Turku 2010).

152. *See also* Risto Riitesuo, *Erottaminen ja kurinpitomenettely yhdistyksessä*, 21 (Helsinki Lakimiesliiton kustannus 2001).

sanction. In Finland, these questions have become relevant after the doping scandal in the Cross-Country Skiing World Championships which were held in Lahti in 2001.

355. Different dimensions can be found when evaluating the lifetime ineligibility sanction in the context of basic rights and fundamental rights. First, it is essential to define the relevant basic right positions which mainly concern the freedom to engage in commercial activity guaranteed in section 18 of the Constitution of Finland, and the protection of property guaranteed in section 15 of the Constitution of Finland. Second, the crucial legal factors relating to a lifetime ineligibility sanction have to be evaluated. The general criteria for the restriction of basic rights, formulated by the Constitutional Law Committee (Parliament of Finland), can function as a useful legal tool in this respect.[153] It is not a question of direct application of these criteria but of taking into account the fundamental requirements of the rule of law. The relevant factors concern, for example, the proportionality principle and the protection under the law.

153. *See*, e.g., Veli-Pekka Viljanen, *Perusoikeuksien rajoitusedellytykset*, 37–64 (Helsinki WSLT 2001).

Chapter 2. Public Regulation

356. In the Finnish legal system, criminal law sanctions are mainly based on the Criminal Code (39/1889). There are only a few sections in the Criminal Code which are especially concerned with sport. Doping offences are the main examples of these sport-related sections. According to section 6, Chapter 44 (Offences endangering health and safety), a person who unlawfully prepares or attempts to prepare a doping substance, imports or attempts to import a doping substance, or sells, conveys, or gives to another, or otherwise disseminates or attempts to disseminate a doping substance, must be sentenced to a fine or to imprisonment for a maximum of two years, unless a more severe penalty for the act has been provided elsewhere in the law, for a doping offence. Additionally, a person who keeps in his or her possession a doping substance with the probable intent to disseminate it unlawfully must be sentenced for a doping offence.

357. If in the doping offence, the offence involves a considerably large amount of doping substances, and considerable financial benefit has been sought, or the offender has acted as a member of a criminal organization that has been specifically organized for the extensive commission of such an offence or the doping substance is disseminated to a minor, and the doping offence is aggravated also when assessed as a whole, the offender must be sentenced for an aggravated doping offence (section 7, Chapter 44) to imprisonment for a minimum sentence of four months and a maximum of four years. If the doping offence, when assessed as a whole, with consideration to the amount of doping substance or to the other circumstances connected with the offence is deemed petty, the offender must be sentenced for a petty doping offence (section 8, Chapter 44) to a fine.

Chapter 3. Private Regulation

§1. Finnish Anti-doping Code

358. The work of anti-doping authorities is a constant struggle against forbidden substances and their methods of use. Reliable testing methods have a central role in this work. High detection level lowers the incentives of athletes and other individuals to use forbidden substances. Furthermore, sanctions have relevance when enforcing anti-doping rules. The end-result can be described as a multiply by these two factors. Both of these factors are relevant in this multiplication. Therefore, it is logical that there have been some changes in the World Anti-Doping Code and in the Finnish Anti-Doping Code concerning sanctions on individuals in cases of anti-doping rule violations. These changes have increased the diversity among sanctions and, at the same, made the sanctions more severe.

359. Sanctions following anti-doping rule violations have a common foundation because the Finnish Anti-Doping Code is based on the World Anti-Doping Code. This has clarified the application of the Finnish Anti-Doping Code. Sanctions have been divided into different categories in the Finnish Anti-Doping Code. According to Article 10.2.1 of the Code, the period of ineligibility shall be four years where the anti-doping rule violation does not involve a specified substance, unless the athlete or other person can establish that the anti-doping rule violation was not intentional, or the anti-doping rule violation involves a specified substance and the anti-doping organization can establish that the anti-doping rule violation was intentional. If Article 10.2.1 does not apply, then period of ineligibility should be two years.

360. For violations of Article 2.3 (Evading, Refusing or Failing to Submit to Sample Collection) or Article 2.5 (Tampering or Attempted Tampering with any part of Doping Control), the period of ineligibility is four years, unless, in the case of failing to submit to sample collection, the athlete can establish that the commission of the anti-doping rule violation was not intentional, in which case the period of ineligibility is for two years. For violations of Article 2.7 (Trafficking or Attempted Trafficking in any Prohibited Substance or Prohibited Method) and Article 2.8 (Administration or Attempted Administration to any Athlete In-Competition of any Prohibited Substance or Prohibited Method, or Administration or Attempted Administration to any Athlete out-of-Competition of any Prohibited Substance or any Prohibited Method that is prohibited Out-of-Competition), the period of ineligibility is a minimum of four years up to lifetime ineligibility.

361. For a second anti-doping rule violation by an athlete or any other person, the period of ineligibility has to be either greater than a six-month period of ineligibility or a period of ineligibility in the range between: (a) the sum of the period of ineligibility imposed for the first anti-doping rule violation plus the period of ineligibility otherwise applicable to the second anti-doping rule violation treated as if it were a first violation, and (b) twice the period of ineligibility otherwise applicable to the second anti-doping rule violation treated as if were the first violation.

362. A third anti-doping rule violation will always result in a lifetime period of ineligibility, except if the third violation fulfils the condition for elimination or reduction of the period of ineligibility under Article 10.5 (Elimination of the Period of Ineligibility where there is No Fault or Negligence) or 10.6 (Reduction of the Period of Ineligibility based on No Significant Fault or Negligence), or involves a violation of Article 2.4 (Whereabouts Failures). In these particular cases, the period of ineligibility shall be from eight years to lifetime ineligibility.

363. The structure and severe nature of sanctions concerning anti-doping rule violations pose challenges for those who apply the above-mentioned anti-doping codes. These codes have to be applied in a coherent way in individual cases. Sanctions imposed by anti-doping organizations need to be justified when taking into account the circumstances in each case. There are many relevant legal questions concerning these sanctions. However, in the following, the relevant questions are mainly evaluated from the perspective of the lifetime ineligibility sanction.

364. Sanctions for a lifetime are only applied in criminal law in Finland. Otherwise, there are no lifetime sanctions in the Finnish legal system. The most interesting legal question concerns the permanence of these sanctions and their legal implications. Therefore, there is a concrete need to evaluate the lifetime ineligibility sanction based on the anti-doping codes in the context of basic rights and human rights. This context can be used to form a legal framework to evaluate the lifetime ineligibility sanction and to give some indications of the future development of the anti-doping codes.

§2. The Finnish Center for Integrity in Sports

365. Clean sport is a common goal for both the government and sports organizations in Finland. In practice, the division of work between the Government and non-governmental organizations is well-established. Basically, the Government has a central role in supporting anti-doping activities financially and developing anti-doping legislation,[154] while the sports federations are responsible for running their own anti-doping programmes. Additionally, concrete measures for eliminating doping are taken by the FINCIS, which is a non-profit organization in Finland.

366. The FINCIS, established in 2016, is in charge of doping control in Finland.[155] Its predecessor, the Finnish Anti-Doping Agency (FINADA), was established in 2001 when there was a strong will to develop doping control in Finland after a number of Finns were found to have used doping agents at the World Ski

154. Various ministries are involved with this work. The Ministry of Social Affairs and Health has a mandate to prepare legislation relating to drugs and the Ministry of Justice is responsible for amending the Criminal Code. The Ministry of Education and Culture promotes anti-doping work generally and supports the Finnish Center for Integrity in Sports financially.

155. *See,* www.suek.fi (accessed 3 May 2021).

Championships that year.[156] The FINCIS carries out testing, promotes anti-doping activities, and supervises compliance with international anti-doping treaties in Finland. The FINCIS is also responsible for implementing international treaties on the manipulation of sports competitions and spectator comfort and safety in Finland.

367. The FINCIS is a non-governmental organization governed by the Finnish Association Act (503/1989) that receives its funding from the Ministry of Education and Culture's lottery funds. It comprises four member organizations: the FOC, the Finnish Paralympic Committee, the Finnish Society of Sports Medicine, and the Government, represented by the Ministry of Education and Culture.

368. In the FINCIS, the board of directors makes budgetary decisions and plans the strategic guidelines. It has a clear mandate based on the rules of the FINCIS to plan, monitor and evaluate anti-doping operations and to grant licences to doping control officers in order to carry out testing. Members of the Board are appointed at the FINCIS annual meeting.

369. The FINCIS has various programmes concerning education for sports and open communication. Its educational programmes are focused on influencing the attitudes of all athletes and sports organizations towards ethics and respect for others. In this way, the FINCIS aims to promote a clean, doping-free, and ethical athletic culture and to increase appreciation for sports.

§3. Enforcement of Anti-doping Codes

370. The FINCIS has an Anti-Doping Hearing Panel as an independent body to investigate doping cases. This Anti-Doping Hearing Panel is appointed by the FINCIS annual meeting. The Anti-Doping Hearing Panel consists of nine members, who are knowledgeable about competitive sports, and two deputy members. The Chairperson, two other members and one deputy member must hold a Master of Laws degree. Three members and one deputy member must be licensed physicians. Additionally, three members must be experts with in-depth knowledge of top-level sports.

371. The Anti-Doping Hearing Panel decides whether the action of an athlete or any other person is to be regarded as an anti-doping rule violation under the Finnish Anti-Doping Code. From 1 January 2021, the Anti-Doping Hearing Panel also has had the duty to make decisions concerning the sanctions to be imposed on individuals and organizations.

156. It is worth noticing that anti-doping work has long roots in Finland: the first national regulations on the use of doping agents were prepared in the 1980s and the National Doping Committee (KDT) was established in 1984. In 1990, doping control was transferred to the Finnish Anti-doping Agency.

372. An athlete or other person can challenge a decision based on the Finnish Anti-Doping Code made by the Anti-Doping Hearing Panel before the Finnish Sports Arbitration Board. In cases involving international-level athletes or international sports events appeals regarding decisions based on Finland's Anti-Doping Rules are submitted to the international CAS.

373. It is highly important that those individuals (athletes and support personnel) who have received a notification of or a request for information on a suspected anti-doping rule violation from FINCIS can have a legal counsellor in anti-doping rule violation proceedings. These services are available through the Finnish Sports Law Association's legal aid system which was taken into use on 1 February 2019. Legal aid is only available in cases of anti-doping rule violations processed in Finland.

374. The rationale of the legal aid system is to provide the services of a legal counsellor with adequate legal expertise at reasonable costs. The legal aid system ensures that processing the anti-doping rule violation is performed fairly and equally to all parties. The system is based on a recommendation issued by the Council of Europe on 20 February 2017.

375. Athletes and support personnel may use the services of a legal counsellor even before the anti-doping rule violation is brought to the Anti-Doping Hearing Panel. This is the case, for example, when an athlete has given a positive A sample in a doping test. The person suspected of committing an anti-doping rule violation can then select their preferred counsellor and contact them about the matter. The counsellor's mandate based on the legal aid system will end after the Anti-Doping Hearing Panel has issued a decision. Therefore, it is not possible to get access to the services of a legal counsellor in order to submit an appeal to the Finnish Sports Arbitration Board through the system.

376. The FINCIS has also a Therapeutic Use Exemption Committee (TUEC) which can, upon written application by an athlete, grant a therapeutic use exemption for a specified time for the use of a prohibited substance and/or a prohibited method in accordance with the International Standard for Therapeutic Use Exemptions approved by WADA.

§4. Lifetime Ineligibility Sanction and Basic Rights

I. Introduction

377. The legal and practical consequences of the ineligibility sanction are defined in Article 10.14 of the Finnish Anti-Doping Code. The main consequence concerns the prohibition against participation during eligibility. No athlete or other person, who has been declared ineligible, may, during the period of ineligibility, participate in any capacity in a competition or activity authorized or organized by any signatory of the World Anti-Doping Code, a signatory's member organization, or a club or other member organization of a signatory's member organization, or in competitions authorized or organized by any professional league or any international- or national-level event organization or any elite or national-level sporting activity funded by a governmental agency.

378. According to Article 10.14.1 of the Finnish Anti-Doping Code, an athlete or other person subject to a period of ineligibility longer than four years may, after completing four years of the period of ineligibility, participate as an athlete in local sports events not sanctioned or otherwise under the jurisdiction of a code signatory or member of a code signatory. However, this is only as long as the local sport event is not at a level that could otherwise qualify the athlete or other person directly or indirectly to compete in a national championship or international event, and does not involve the athlete or other person working in any capacity with protected persons.

379. Article 10.14.3 of the Finnish Anti-Doping Code, where an athlete or other person, who has been declared ineligible, violates the prohibition against participation during the ineligible period, the results of such participation will be further disqualified, and a new period of ineligibility equal in length to the original period of ineligibility will be added to the end of the original period of ineligibility.

380. The scope of the ineligibility sanction is very wide. In practice, the ineligibility sanction covers all relevant actions in sports organizations and sports competitions. A person who has been declared ineligible cannot engage in sporting activities as an athlete, a coach, a doctor, or an official. From the perspective of basic rights, the ineligibility sanction concerns, primarily, everyone's right to earn his or her livelihood by the employment, occupation, or commercial activity of his or her choice and this is protected in section 17 of the Constitution of Finland. The freedom to engage in commercial activity can be relevant to all the functional roles described earlier.

381. The ineligibility sanction has its closest connections to an athlete's right to earn his or her livelihood by employment, occupation, or commercial activity.[157] The ineligibility sanction prevents athletes from participating in sports competitions and, thus, their opportunity to earn a living by these means. Additionally, the ineligibility sanction at least leads to a radical reduction of incomes related to sporting activities, such as incomes based on sponsorship agreements.

382. In practice, the lifetime ineligibility sanction terminates an athlete's professional career. In this respect, the difference between the lifetime ineligibility sanction and long ineligibility sanctions is marginal because athletes' careers are, by definition, short and it is not easy to return to professional sport after a long ineligibility period. However, it is essential for an athlete that the ineligibility sanction

157. *See*, e.g., Olli Rauste, *Urheiluoikeus*, 170–172 (Helsinki Lakimiesliiton Kustannus 1997). *See also* KKO 1998:122.

covers any activities organized by sports federations and other organizations including coaching and other relevant activities. The lifetime ineligibility sanction can, in practice, prevent former athletes from earning their living by many parallel ways.

383. The lifetime ineligibility sanction can also concern other individuals than athletes, such as coaches, doctors, and other officials. Typically, the careers of coaches, doctors, and other officials are much longer than those of athletes. Therefore, the practical consequences of the lifetime ineligibility sanction are particularly harsh in these cases. Ultimately, the lifetime ineligibility sanction can terminate a professional career of a coach or a doctor.

384. It also has to be noticed that prohibited association is sanctioned in the Finnish Anti-Doping Code. According to Article 2.10 of the Code, association by an athlete or other person subject to the authority of an anti-doping organization in a professional or sport-related capacity with any athlete support person who is serving a period of ineligibility if subject to the authority of an anti-doping organization is forbidden. The same also concerns association by an athlete or other person subject to the authority of an anti-doping organization in a professional or sport-related capacity with any athlete support person who has been convicted or found in a criminal, disciplinary or professional proceeding to have engaged in conduct which would have constituted a violation of anti-doping rules if code-compliant rules had been applicable to such person.[158]

385. The interface between the ineligibility sanction and the freedom to engage in commercial activity guaranteed in the Constitution of Finland is evident when the right of athletes, coaches or other individuals to earn their livelihood is restricted in sport. However, it is possible to evaluate this interface in a wider context. The actions and practices of a sports federation can enhance the practical consequences of the ineligibility sanction to the legal position of an individual athlete. In practice, this concerns the freedom of a sports federation to refer to the ineligibility sanction in a single case and choose its contracting parties. Legal evaluation has to be focused on the effects of the freedom to engage in commercial activity which are based on practices and restrictions driven by a sports federation in order to prevent cooperation with a person who has been declared ineligible or his company.[159]

386. The above-mentioned legal question has to be evaluated in conjunction with the legal status of a sports federation. The protection of property, guaranteed in section 15 of the Constitution of Finland, covers both the protection of the property everyone already has and the freedom of contract.[160] This legal background means that everyone should, in principle, have the right to choose his or her contracting

158. The rule concerns any athlete support person, even if the person is not subject to the authority of an anti-doping organization and where ineligibility has not been addressed in a results management process pursuant to the World Anti-Doping Code.
159. *See*, e.g., The Finnish Sports Arbitration Board, Decision 16/2008.
160. *See*, e.g., Pekka Länsineva, *Perusoikeudet ja varallisuussuhteet*, 182–183 (Helsinki Suomalainen Lakimiesyhdistys 2001).

partners and the terms used in his or her contracts.[161] However, the relevant context has to be taken into consideration when applying the rights guaranteed in the Constitution of Finland. In a relationship between a sports federation and a person who has been declared ineligible, the crucial legal question concerns the horizontal effect of basic rights.[162] It has to be evaluated how exercising one's right might affect others' legal positions and freedoms. Based on its rules, a sports federation can collectively regulate conditions for engaging in commercial activities within sports competitions the federation organizes.

387. In these cases, it has to be noticed that restrictions on the freedom to engage in commercial activities are not directly based on the ineligibility sanction but on the fact that a sports federation refers to this sanction when making contracts. The connection between the ineligibility sanction and the commercial activity in question is not irrelevant when evaluating the above-mentioned question from the perspective of basic rights. Neither should the competence of sports federations to collectively regulate conditions for engaging in commercial activities be ignored in the evaluation.

388. In principle, this competence does not preclude the possibility that a sports federation can refuse to make a contract with a person who has been declared ineligible or place conditions on the cooperation. However, these decisions must have a legitimate basis. A sports federation can refer to the ineligibility sanction when making its decision. A legitimate aim can be, for example, to avoid speculations that a sports federation is not obeying the ineligibility sanction or is trying to circumvent the practical consequences of the sanction.

389. In any case, measures taken by a sports federation should be proportionate. The proportionate principle requires a decent discretion based on the facts of each case. Restrictions following these measures should be evaluated in different dimensions (personal, material and temporal). If the relevant requirements based on the proportionality principle are not met, measures taken by a sports federation can be evaluated, for example, in context with the prohibition of the abuse of rights.[163]

390. The lifetime ineligibility sanction is a peculiar legal phenomenon, which can have various effects on the legal position of an athlete or a person who has been declared ineligible for their lifetime.[164] These effects should be evaluated in a comprehensive way. Evaluation should cover both direct and indirect effects. Decisions made by a sports federation or other sports organization can, in practice, enhance these effects dramatically. In practice, these decisions can prevent an athlete or any

---

161. *See*, e.g., Pertti Juhani Muukkonen, *Sopimusvapauden käsitteestä*, Lakimies, 601, 607 (1956).
162. *See* generally Veli-Pekka Viljanen, *Ulottuuko perusoikeuksien vaikutus yksityisoikeudellisiin oikeussuhteisiin?*, 273–279 (in Ari Saarnilehto (ed.), Juhlajulkaisu Allan Huttunen 1928 – 5/11 – 1988, Turun yliopiston oikeustieteellisen tiedekunnan julkaisuja A. Juhlajulkaisut N:o 2, (Turku 1988)).
163. *See* Antti Aine, *Kilpailu ja sopimus*, 382–390 (Helsinki Suomalainen Lakimiesyhdistys 2011).
164. *See also* Mikko Nisula, *Perusoikeudet suomalaisessa doping-prosessissa*, 48 (Turun yliopiston oikeustieteellisen tiedekunnan julkaisuja, Urheiluoikeuden sarja 3, Turku 2003).

other person from engaging in commercial activities or make it extremely difficult within a sport sanctioned by a sports federation.

II. Application

391. Fundamental legal questions between the legal position of athletes and the anti-doping system are touched upon when evaluating the lifetime ineligibility sanction within the context of basic rights. It might even be possible to consider whether the lifetime ineligibility sanction is justified at all from this perspective. However, it is not wise to just concentrate on this question. On the contrary, it should be evaluated how ineligibility sanctions and, especially, the lifetime ineligibility sanction can be applied in a coherent way in concrete cases.

392. Evaluation of the interface between the lifetime ineligibility sanction and basic rights should be comprehensive and systematic. This requirement is justified because the lifetime ineligibility sanction has wide effects on an athlete's legal position and rights. Evaluation can be based on the general criteria concerning the restriction of basic rights formulated by the Constitutional Law Committee (Parliament of Finland).

393. These criteria form a solid legal structure on which the balancing of different rights of individuals and collective goods is based. It is not a question of direct application of these criteria but elaborating on the relevant legal factors presented in the restriction test. The general criteria concerning the restriction of basic rights do not give direct answers to legal problems, but they help to direct the evaluation into relevant aspects of legal problems. The material basis for the evaluation has to be seen in connection with the legal background of each case.

394. The general criteria concerning the restriction of basic rights form a whole. In principle, all the criteria should be applied in each case.[165] However, different criteria can have different relational weights in concrete cases. There can also be overlapping areas between different criteria.[166]

395. First, it is essential to define the purposes that the anti-doping codes support. This evaluation is closely connected to the justified cause for restricting basic rights in these cases. Second, the proportionality principle has a central role when evaluating the lifetime ineligibility sanction.[167] Measures taken to ensure anti-doping compliance may not go beyond what is necessary for achieving the aim pursued. Restrictions following the lifetime ineligibility sanction should be necessary, which means in particular, that there are no other less-restricting options available.

---

165. *See* Veli-Pekka Viljanen, *Perusoikeuksien rajoitusedellytykset*, 61 (Helsinki WSLT 2001).
166. *See* Viljanen, *supra* note 164, at 80.
167. *See also* Jari Eskuri, *Urheilijaa suojaavat perusoikeudet*, 47–50 (Turun yliopiston oikeustieteellisen tiedekunnan julkaisuja, Urheiluoikeuden sarja 10, Turku 2005).

Third, it should be evaluated how precise the anti-doping code is and how legal protection, for example, through appeal procedures, is organized.

396. The requirement of a justified cause for the restriction forms an initial starting point for the evaluation. The restriction should be based on a strong societal need. This criterion can be evaluated in different contexts. Requirements for a justified cause can also be assessed in conjunction with the protection of other athletes' basic rights. The anti-doping codes promote athletes' health because harmful substances and methods are prohibited in sport. In fact, the ineligibility sanction based on the anti-doping codes protects the opportunities for athletes to use their rights in a meaningful way in sport. Doping has harmful effects on workable competitive conditions in sport. The anti-doping codes have a close connection to formal justice, which refers to the idea that every athlete should have an equal opportunity to his or her rights in sports competitions; thus winning should not require using prohibited substances or methods.

397. Alternatively, the restriction of basic rights can be based on achieving important societal goals that have a close connection to the Constitution of Finland or, at least, have institutional support in the Constitution.[168] Generally, the legitimate aims of the anti-doping codes concern promoting public health. From the societal perspective, it is illegitimate to promote sporting activities in which winning requires athletes to use prohibited substances or methods. From an internal perspective, the anti-doping codes support fair play in sport. The concept of fair play is multidimensional but it can be seen, in the current context, to refer to equal opportunities for all athletes in sports competitions without using prohibited substances or methods of enhancement.

398. The requirement of a justified cause for the restriction has to be evaluated separately concerning every relevant basic right.[169] The evaluation should especially concern the freedom to engage in commercial activity guaranteed in section 18 of the Constitution of Finland and the protection of property guaranteed in section 15 of the Constitution of Finland. The relevant factors in the evaluation are extremely similar.

399. Basic rights have an initial starting point in the evaluation. The one who refers to the legitimate cause for the restriction has the initial burden of proof. At the same time, it has to be remembered that the protection of basic rights is, in most cases, relational. Basic rights and their use can be regulated. This follows from the collective background of basic rights. Individuals have to take into consideration other individuals and the above-mentioned societal goals when using their basic rights.

---

168. *See also* Veli-Pekka Viljanen, *Perusoikeuksien rajoitusedellytykset*, 184 (Helsinki WSLT 2001).

169. *See* Veli-Pekka Viljanen, *Perusoikeuksien soveltamisala, Perusoikeuksien rajoittaminen*, 154–157 (in Pekka Hallberg, Heikki Karapuu, Tuomas Ojanen, Martin Scheinin, Kaarlo Tuori & Veli-Pekka Viljanen (eds), Perusoikeudet, 2nd ed., Helsinki WSOYpro 2011).

400. The proportionality principle forms a central dimension when evaluating the lifetime ineligibility sanction within the context of basic rights. There are three parts in the evaluation. First, the restriction should have a justified basis. Discretion is closely linked to the purposes of the anti-doping codes. Second, the restriction should be necessary to realize a justified aim. In practice, this means that there is, realistically, no other way to achieve this aim. Third, the restriction should be proportionate.[170]

401. The proportionality principle leads to a balancing of the different societal interests with each other.[171] This balancing operation can be practised on a general level, but it also has relevance in concrete cases. Typically, the aims of the juridical regulation and the special features of each context are relevant when applying legal norms in individual cases. The discretion related to these cases is by its nature multidimensional. The proportionality principle forms a solid legal structure for this discretion.

402. The relevant context has to be taken into consideration when applying the proportionality principle.[172] The ineligibility sanction concerns athletes, coaches, and other officials: in principle, these individuals are at the centre when applying basic rights and are presumed to have the strongest need for legal protection in these cases. At the same time, athletes and coaches are often professionals, and it is also reasonable to assume that entrepreneurs are able to carry the risks related to their commercial activities.

403. Additionally, the forbidden nature of the activities in question is also relevant in the legal discretion. Practices against the fair play principle do not require strong legal protection. However, it has to be remembered that the ineligibility sanction has wide effects on the future prospects of an athlete or a coach to engage in commercial activities which might have an indirect connection to the use of prohibited substances or methods.

404. The societal importance of the cause for the restriction is relevant when applying the proportionality principle. The purposes of the sanctions enforced by the anti-doping codes and anti-doping rules are justified because they concern, in general, the protection of fair play and the athlete's right to participate in doping-free sport. The ineligibility sanction can be said to advance these purposes.

405. Sanctions based on the anti-doping codes have effects which are related both to specific deterrence and to general deterrence. The ineligibility sanction prevents an athlete, a coach or any other person who has been declared ineligible to participate in any capacity in a competition or activity authorized by any sports organization. In principle, sanctions take away the ability of athletes, coaches and

---

170. *See*, e.g., PeVM 25/1994 vp, p. 5, ja HE 309/1993 vp, p. 30.
171. *See* Veli-Pekka Viljanen, *Perusoikeuksien rajoitusedellytykset*, 210–211 (Helsinki WSLT 2001).
172. *See also* Jani Pitkänen, *Urheilun kurinpitoseuraamusten mittaaminen*, 35–40 (Turun yliopiston oikeustieteellisen tiedekukunnan julkaisuja, Urheiluoikeuden julkaisusarja 35, Turku 2012).

any other person to commit such acts during the period of ineligibility. Moreover, the opportunity to impose sanctions also generally decreases the incentives of individuals to violate the anti-doping codes. Therefore, the ineligibility sanctions have general preventive effects. The severity of the sanction is one aspect which is relevant when evaluating the general prevention of anti-doping violations.

406. The lifetime ineligibility sanction, as the most severe sanction in anti-doping rule violation cases, has an evident preventive effect. However, it has to be remembered that the smooth functioning of the anti-doping codes and their application is not just based on severe sanctions. The certainty of sanctioning is also relevant. A typical feature of a workable anti-doping system is the combination of justified sanctions and the relevant certainty of sanctioning. A critical part of anti-doping codes and their application has long been related to difficulties in the methods of establishing anti-doping rule violations. Despite these difficulties, a sustainable strategy cannot be based only on severe sanctions. Otherwise, there will be various legal problems to be solved in individual cases.

407. Different dimensions of the restriction of basic rights have to be evaluated when applying the proportionality principle. It has to be evaluated how wide and deep the restrictive effects are on an individual's rights. In the evaluation, a relevant factor can, for example, concern those options which an individual has to arrange for his or her activities. Restriction should be necessary in order to achieve a justified societal goal.

408. The lifetime ineligibility sanction has strong effects on an athlete's or other person's legal position. It is possible to argue that based on these effects the lifetime ineligibility sanction should be abolished. If this is not possible in practice, it should be developed, at least, in two ways. Specified juridical mechanisms should be created for individual cases when making decisions concerning the evaluation and end of the lifetime ineligibility sanction.[173]

409. It is a basic legal requirement that all the relevant procedures are defined in the anti-doping codes. This requirement is closely linked to the basic premises of the rule of law. Everyone should have a right to make a decision pertaining to his or her rights or obligations reviewed by a court of law or other independent organ for the administration of justice. This right is protected in section 21 of the Constitution of Finland and in the international treaties on human rights. The procedure must fulfil the fundamental requirements of a fair trial as defined in Article 6 of the European Convention on Human Rights.

410. Even after the adoption of the World Anti-Doping Code 2021, the legal status of the lifetime ineligibility sanction can be evaluated in individual cases before a court of law or in an arbitration proceeding, although the appellate bodies in sport, such as the Finnish Sports Arbitration Board, are also competent to handle these

173. *See also* Jari Eskuri, *Urheilijaa suojaavat perusoikeudet*, 49 (Turun yliopiston oikeustieteellisen tiedekunnan julkaisuja, Urheiluoikeuden sarja 10, Turku 2005).

cases. However, the severity of the consequences following the lifetime ineligibility sanction requires that concrete legal rules concerning the relevant procedure must be enacted.

411. There are many important legal questions which have to be regulated by the proposed rule. One of these questions concerns the minimum period of time after which the legal status of the lifetime ineligibility sanction can be evaluated. It is not a justified situation that, in practice, all the above-mentioned procedures are currently based on an ad hoc evaluation in each case. Evidently, it takes time before a solid case law can be developed. Concrete changes are needed in the anti-doping codes in order to protect the rights of athletes, coaches, and other individuals in these cases.

412. Legal norms regulating the lifetime ineligibility sanction should be precise. In practice, this means that, for example, aggravating circumstances, which may increase the period of ineligibility, should be defined in the anti-doping codes. It is evident though that no definite rules can be adopted. However, even some guidelines would enhance the development of a coherent case law. From the perspective of an appeal body or a court of law, it is essential to have some guidelines to apply when evaluating a single case. Such proposed guidelines could, for their part, increase the predictability of the decisions made in these proceedings.

III. Conclusion

413. Legal evaluation of the lifetime ineligibility sanction is by its nature comprehensive, which means that all relevant arguments have to be taken into consideration. In principle, anti-doping organizations have the burden of establishing why the ineligibility sanction should be sustained in an individual case. However, an athlete or other individual who has been declared ineligible for their lifetime has to present concrete evidence of the effects of the sanction on his basic rights. A court of law or an appellate body in sport has a duty to give reasons for its decision, which is not always an easy task. Decisions made in these cases are by their nature juridical, although different aspects concerning the legal position of an athlete and the purposes of the anti-doping codes should be balanced against each other.

414. The proportionality principle has a central role in this balancing. The severity of each anti-doping rule violation has to be evaluated and the harmful effects of each violation have to be analysed. The relevant factors concern not only the facts of an individual case but all aspects related to general deterrence also have to be taken into consideration.

415. Several factors can be relevant when applying the proportionality test and some examples can be given. It is significant whether an athlete or other person has committed an anti-doping rule violation as part of a doping plan or scheme individually, or been involved in a conspiracy or a common enterprise to commit the anti-doping rule violations. Likewise, it is relevant whether an athlete or other person has engaged in deceptive or obstructing conduct to avoid the detection or adjunction of an anti-doping rule violation.

416. Arguments for sustaining the lifetime ineligibility sanction in an individual case have to be evaluated together with the restrictions following the lifetime ineligibility sanction. Different dimensions of the restriction have to be evaluated. These dimensions concern the personal, material, and temporal scope of the restrictions.

417. It is evident that a long ineligibility period enhances the restrictive effects of the sanction. At the same time, the factual effects of the lifetime ineligibility sanction on the ability of an athlete or other person to engage in commercial activities have to be assessed. In practice, the decisions made by sports organizations can enhance these effects. Additionally, the effects following the lifetime ineligibility sanction on other persons than the one who has been declared ineligible have to be analysed. These effects are highly relevant when they affect the opportunities of family members and other relatives to engage in commercial activities related to sport.

418. The lifetime ineligibility sanction can be evaluated critically from the perspective of basic rights. The critical aspects concern the permanent nature of the lifetime ineligibility sanction. This dimension, together with its wide material scope, can lead to restrictions on basic rights which can be legally challenged. It would be wise to have an open discussion on whether the lifetime ineligibility sanction could be abolished. If this is not possible based on the peculiarities of the relevant context, legal mechanisms and procedures must be created in the anti-doping codes as regards how to evaluate the legality of the lifetime ineligibility sanction in individual cases. Simultaneously, criteria for the evaluation of aggravating circumstances, which may increase the period of ineligibility, should be defined in the anti-doping codes. These criteria cannot be defined as strict rules. They are guidelines, which enhance the practical prospect of applying the anti-doping codes in a systematic way.

419. Anti-doping organizations and sports organizations have different strategies when evaluating the future development of the lifetime ineligibility sanction. The above-mentioned legal aspects are in favour of a proactive strategy, which tries to prevent legal problems from occurring. However, it is possible that the relationship between the lifetime ineligibility sanction and basic rights is only evaluated in case law. This option can lead to inconsistency in case law and cases where the legality of the lifetime ineligibility sanction is challenged. These risks can be managed, but it requires systematic steps taken by anti-doping organizations and sports organizations.

Part IV. Sport and Commerce

Chapter 1. Competition Law

§1. Introduction

420. Competition law can be divided into two parts: conduct control and structural control. Conduct control deals with cartels and abuse of dominant market positions. Structural control covers mergers and concentrations. In the following, the evaluation will concentrate on the relationship between conduct control norms and sport. Merger cases will be referred to in certain circumstances.[174]

421. Competition law has long traditions in Finland. There have been several stages in the development of the relevant legislation since the 1950s.[175] Currently, the Competition Act (948/2011) forms the most important part of the legislation. According to section 5 of the Competition Act, all agreements between undertakings, decisions by associations of undertakings, and concerted practices by undertakings, which have as their object the significant prevention, restriction or distortion of competition or which result in a significant prevention, restriction, or distortion of competition are prohibited. In particular, this prohibition concerns agreements, decisions, or practices which:

(1) directly or indirectly fix purchase or selling prices or any other trading conditions;
(2) limit or control production, markets, technical development or investment;
(3) share markets or sources of supply;
(4) apply dissimilar conditions to equivalent transactions with other trading partners, thereby placing them at a competitive disadvantage; or

174. The relationship between economic activity relating to sport and merger control rules has been of special concern to the media sector. The Commission has made many decisions in merger cases where one of the parties has been a company owning media rights to sports events. *See*, e.g., the following Decisions No. Comp/M.2876 – *Newcorp / Telepiù*, 2.4.2003, No. Comp/Jv.37 – *B Sky B – Kirch Pay TV*, 21.3.2000, No. IV/M.779 – *Bertelsmann / CLT*, 7.10.1996, No. IV/M.1327 – *NC / Canal + / CDPQ / Bank America*, 3.12.1998, ja No. IV/M.110 – *ABC / Generale Des eaux / Canal + / W.H. Smith TV*, 10.9.1991.

175. *See also* Antti Aine, *Suomen kilpailulainsäädännön kehityspiirteitä*, 5–31 (in Antti Aine & Anne Kumpula (eds), Kansainvälisestä kaupasta. Juhlajulkaisu Tuula Ämmälä (Turku University of Turku 2000)).

(5) make the conclusion of a contract subject to acceptance by the other party of supplementary obligations which, by their nature or according to the commercial usage, have no connection with the subject of such a contract.

422. Section 6 of the Competition Act concerns exemptions to section 5. The prohibition of section 5 does not apply to any agreement between undertakings, any decision by an association of undertakings or any concerted practice by undertakings or any category of agreements, decisions or concerted practices which:

(1) contributes to improving the production or distribution of goods or to promoting technical or economic progress;
(2) allows consumers a fair share of the resulting benefit;
(3) does not impose on the undertakings concerning restraints which are not indispensable to the attainment of those objectives; and
(4) does not afford such undertakings the possibility of eliminating competition in respect of a substantial part of the products in question.

423. Section 7 of the Competition Act concerns the abuse of dominant market positions. According to this section, any abuse by one or more undertakings or association of undertakings of a dominant market position must be prohibited. Abuse may, in particular, consist of:

(1) directly or indirectly imposing unfair purchase or selling prices or other unfair trading conditions;
(2) limiting production, markets, or technical developments to the prejudice of consumers;
(3) applying dissimilar conditions to equivalent transactions with trading partners, thereby placing them at a competitive disadvantage;
(4) making the conclusion of a contract subject to acceptance by the other contract party of supplementary obligations which, by their nature or according to commercial usage, have no connection with the subject of such a contract.

424. Sections 5, 6 and 7 have close material connections to Articles 101 and 102 TFEU. In point of fact, the conduct control norms in the Finnish Competition Restriction Act were harmonized on 1 May 2004 to correspond to Articles 101 and 102 TFEU.[176] According to the *travaux préparatoires*, the case law based on Articles 101 and 102 TFEU should be taken into consideration when applying our national norms.[177] Therefore, Articles 101 and 102 TFEU and case law concerning these articles are relevant when evaluating the relationship between Finnish competition law and sport.

---

176. The only difference concerns naturally the requirement 'effect on trade between Member States' which defines the boundary between conduct, which is subject to Community law, and conduct which is governed solely by national law.
177. HE 11/2004 vp, 31, 33 and 35.

425. Articles 101 and 102 TFEU form the core of EU competition law. Article 101(1) TFEU prohibits all agreements between undertakings, decisions by associations of undertakings and concerted practices that may affect trade between Member States and which have as their object or effect the prevention, restriction, or distortion of competition within the Internal Market. Article 102 TFEU provides that an abuse by one or more undertakings of a dominant position within the Common Market, or in a substantial part thereof, is to be prohibited in so far as it may affect trade between Member States.

426. It is worth noticing that the enforcement of Articles 101 and 102 changed radically on 1 May 2004, when the new enforcement Regulation 1/2003 came into force. The central feature of the new regulation is the direct applicability of Article 101(3) TFEU (i.e., the exemption clause). After the reform, undertakings are obliged to examine and appraise their agreements to ensure their compatibility with the competition rules. The reform has increased the importance of competition law risk management. This matter is vitally important to firms because the sanctions of breaching competition law are substantial (penalty payments and periodic penalty payments, a nullity sanction and damages).[178]

§2. Competition Law and Sport

I. General

427. The application of Articles 101 and 102 TFEU to sporting activity can be described as consisting of interrelated layers of criteria. First, the relationship between the general scope of EU competition law and sport has to be considered. The starting point is the question of whether sport constitutes an economic activity or not, or in other words, is there a distinction between purely sporting interests and economic activity? For an activity to belong within the general scope of EU competition law, it has to restrict competition within the meaning of Article 101(1) or 102 TFEU. In the case of an agreement between undertakings that has restrictive effects on competition, a decision has to be made about whether an agreement can benefit from the exemption in Article 101(3) TFEU. If these criteria for exemption are fulfilled, an agreement is allowed under EU competition law.

428. EU competition law rules are not applied in a vacuum, on the contrary, the actual context has to be taken into consideration. The special features of sport can affect the application of EU competition law at every stage previously mentioned. The effect that sport and its special features can have on the application of EU competition law rules will be discussed in greater detail in the following.

178. According to s. 13 of the Finnish Competition Act, a penalty payment imposed on an undertaking can be 10% of its total turnover in the preceding business year.

II. Purely Sporting Interests and Economic Activity

429. According to the relevant case law, the practice of sport is subject to EU competition law only so far as it constitutes an economic activity within the meaning of Article 2 of the EC Treaty. The basic criteria were set by the European Court of Justice (ECJ) in a case involving free movement.[179] In this case, a distinction was made between purely sporting interests and an economic activity. The ECJ followed its previous case law in the Dona case, which concerned the rules of a sporting organization that limited the right of professional or semi-professional players to take part in football matches.[180] The ECJ stated that the EC Treaty does not prevent the adoption of rules or practices that exclude foreign players from participation in certain matches for reasons which are not economic in nature, and which relate to the particular nature and context of such matches and are thus of sporting interest only (e.g., matches between national teams from different countries). These restrictions on the scope of the provisions in question must, however, remain limited to their proper objective.

430. The EGC has followed the above-mentioned reasoning in its case law: *Meca-Medina and Majcen v. the Commission* concerned the relationship between the anti-doping rules of the IOC and the International Swimming Federation and Articles 101 and 102 TFEU.[181] The EGC stated that purely sporting rules, which have nothing to do with the economic relationships of competition, do not fall within the scope of Articles 101 and 102 TFEU. The EGC further stated that the situation would change if those rules were applied in a discriminatory manner. In *Laurent Piau v. the Commission*, the EGC decided that Federation Internationale de Football Association (FIFA) was acting as an association of economic undertakings when it adopted the Players' Agents Regulations.[182] The scope of EU competition law covers these rules.

431. The ECJ clarified the relevant case law in *Meca-Medina and Majcen v. the Commission* when it overturned the previous decision of the EGC.[183] According to the ECJ, the fact that sporting rules do not constitute restrictions on freedom of movement, because they concern questions of purely sporting interest and have nothing to do with economic activity, 'means neither that the sporting activity in question necessarily falls outside the scope of Articles 101 and 102 TFEU nor that the rules do not satisfy the specific requirements of those articles'.[184] This decision involves an important change in the development of case law. The decisive point is

179. Case 36/74, *Walrave and Koch v. Association Union cycliste internationale*, ECR 1974 1405, paras 4–8.
180. Case 13/76, *Doná v. Mantero*, ECR 1976 1333, paras 12–14.
181. Case T-313/02, *Meca-Medina and Majcen v. the Commission*, (2004) ECR II 3291.
182. Case T-193/02, *Laurent Piau v. the Commission,* (2005) ECR II 209.
183. Case C-519/04 P, *Meca-Medina and Majcen v. the Commission*, (2004) ECR II 3291.
184. Case C-519/04 P, *Meca-Medina and Majcen v. the Commission*, (2004) ECR II 3291, para. 31.

no longer whether a sporting activity deals with purely sporting interests. The difficulties surrounding the separation of the economic aspects from the sporting aspects of a sport can be avoided. The application criteria for Articles 101 and 102 TFEU must now be considered.

432. The central application criterion deals with the definition of an undertaking. Articles 101 and 102 TFEU apply only to undertakings. An undertaking is basically defined in the same way under Articles 101 and 102. The definition of an undertaking has been established by case law. No direct comparison can be made between the definition of an undertaking in the context of EU competition law and that in other legislation (e.g., company law). The term undertaking refers to an economic entity in EU competition law. It is essential that the undertaking should carry on some economic or commercial activity; the legal status or the way the economic entity is financed is not the decisive matter.[185] The term covers, for example, limited liability companies, trade associations, and self-employed professionals.

433. The application of the concept of an undertaking to sports activities can be used for an individual athlete, a sports club, or a sports federation. A professional athlete can be regarded as an undertaking.[186] In this sense, a professional athlete can be considered as being equivalent to a performing artist who is regarded as an undertaking if he engages in economic or commercial activity in his own right. An undertaking is basically an independent market actor.

434. A sports club can be seen as an undertaking when it engages in economic activities in its own name.[187] In practice, engaging in economic activities can mean, for example, providing sports entertainment services for consumers, sponsors, and media companies. The status of sports federations in the competition law context can be defined in the same way.[188] These organizations very often wield significant power in matters which have considerable economic consequences (e.g., joint selling of media rights) and affect other undertakings. In these circumstances, the actions of sports federations are considered as falling within the scope of EU competition rules. The facts of each case affect the way in which the legal status of sports federations is legally constructed. In some cases, national sports federations have been regarded as individual undertakings.[189] While in other cases, national sports federations have been seen as associations of undertakings, and international sports federations as associations of associations of undertakings.[190]

---

185. *See*, e.g., C-41/90, *Höfner and Elser v. Macrotron GmbH*, ECR 1991 1979, para. 21.
186. *See*, e.g., Opinion of Advocate General Cosmas in joined cases C-51/96 and 191/97, *Cristelle Deliége v. Asbl Ligue Francophone de judo et disciplines associées*, (2000) ECR I 2549, and Olli Rauste, *Urheiluoikeus*, 76 (Helsinki Lakimiesliiton Kustannus 1997).
187. *See*, e.g., Opinion of Advocate General Lenz in Case C-415/93, *Union royale belge des societes de football association ASBL et al. v. Bosman*, ECR 1995 I 4921, para. 255.
188. *See*, e.g., Opinion of Advocate General Lenz in Case C-415/93, *Union royale belge des societes de football association ASBL v. Bosman*, ECR 1995 I 4921, para. 256.
189. Case T-193/02, *Laurent Piau v. the Commission*, (2005) ECR II 209.
190. Commission Decision 23.7.2003 Comp/C.2-37.398 – Joint selling of the commercial rights of the UEFA Champions League, para. 109.

III. Special Characteristics of Sport and EU Competition Law

435. Sport possesses some unusual characteristics that distinguish it from normal commercial sectors. These special characteristics can be taken into consideration when applying EU competition rules, and the role of these special characteristics has been approved in case law. Article 165 TFEU strengthens the institutional position of these characteristics when it refers to the European dimension in sport.

436. The key feature of the sports market is associated with an interdependence of interests between participants in sporting competition. Athletes and clubs need other athletes and clubs to provide sports services. The functioning of the sports markets is largely based on a certain degree of equality between clubs and the uncertainty of results. This matter has a great impact on the value of sports services. It is typical of sports markets that participants have to control the differences between themselves in order to guarantee the uncertainty of results.

437. The ECJ recognized the special characteristics of sport in its famous Bosman decision.[191] The ECJ noticed the considerable social importance which sporting activities have in the EU. According to the ECJ, the aim of maintaining a balance between clubs by preserving a certain degree of equality must be accepted as legitimate. However, the critical point is concerned with the means by which this legitimate aim can be achieved. What has to be considered is whether the effects of restrictive competition are inherent in the pursuit of this objective and are proportionate. Inherency and proportionality have strengthened their position as the central criteria after the Meca-Medina judgment of the ECJ.[192]

438. Aims other than maintaining a balance between clubs can have relevance when applying EU competition rules. One example that can be mentioned is the aim of encouraging recruitment and training of young players, which was recognized by the ECJ in the Bosman judgment.[193] The range of valid aims depends greatly on the special features of every sports market.

439. In practice, the special characteristics of sport can be relevant in the application of Articles 101(1) and 102 TFEU or when exempting a contract provision under Article 101(3) TFEU. This is a question of the overall context. Agreements

---

191. Case C-415/93, *Union royale belge des societes de football association ASBL v. Bosman,* (1995) ECR I 4921, para. 106.
192. Case C-519/04 P, *Meca-Medina and Majcen v. the Commission*, (2006) ECR I 6991.
193. Case C-415/93, *Union royale belge des societes de football association ASBL v. Bosman*, (1995) ECR I 4921, para. 106. *See also* Stephen Weatherill, *Do Sporting Associations Make 'Law' or Are They Merely Subject to It?*, 9(7/8) Eur. Bus. L. Rev. 220 (1998), which implies an uncertain attitude towards the aim of encouraging recruitment and training of young players as a specific characteristics for sport.

restricting competition might be inherent and proportionate in order to achieve legitimate aims related to sports activities.[194]

440. The special characteristics of sport may lead to the conclusion that an agreement, which restricts the freedom of action of one or both parties, does not fall within the prohibitions laid down in Article 101(1) or 102 TFEU.[195] The doctrine of ancillary restraints may be mentioned here. This doctrine covers restrictions which are imperative to the achievement of legitimate objectives and are proportionate to these objectives. The Commission stated in the Union of European Football Associations (UEFA) case that the UEFA rule 'Integrity of the UEFA Club competitions: Independence of clubs' is a decision taken by an association of associations of undertakings within the meaning of Article 101 TFEU.[196] The Commission's view was that this UEFA rule was not prohibited by Article 101(1) because its object was not to restrict competition, and the limitation of freedom of action of clubs and investors that it entailed was inherent to the very existence of UEFA competitions. There was no need for an exemption under Article 101(3).

441. The above-mentioned decision of the Commission can be seen as a statement which emphasizes the importance of context when applying Articles 101 and 102 TFEU. The object of an agreement cannot be set aside when the restrictive effects on competition are assessed. In this case, the Commission pointed out the relationship between ownership restrictions and the proper functioning of the market. The special characteristics of sport occupy a central position in this assessment. The Commission referred to the fairness and honesty of sporting competition as an essential precondition for the proper functioning of the market. The Commission also stated that the sporting rule is necessary and proportionate in order to maintain the public's confidence in the fairness and authenticity of the game.

442. The special characteristics of sport can affect the decision to apply the exemption clause under Article 101(3) TFEU. The necessity of the exemption can be argued on the basis of these characteristics. An example of this is the Commission's decision concerning the joint selling of the commercial rights to the UEFA Champions League. The Commission stated in its assessment of the agreement's restrictive effects on competition that because of the special characteristics of sport, there is, for example, a possible need to protect weaker clubs through a cross-subsidization of funds from the richer to the poorer clubs. The Commission noted in its decision that the joint selling agreement had restrictive effects on competition

194. *See*, e.g., the Opinion of Advocate General Alber in Case C-176/96, *Lehtonen and Castors Canada Dry Namur-Braine v. Fédération royale belge des sociétés de Basketball et Asbl Basket Liga-ligue Basket Belgium*, (2000) ECR I 2681.
195. *See also* Jens Pelle van der Brinck, *E.C. Competition Law and the Regulation of Football: Part II*, 21(9) Eur. Competition L. Rev. 421 (2000).
196. Case Comp/37 806: ENIC/UEFA.

which were not necessary under the terms of Article 101(1) TFEU. The Commission stated explicitly that the special characteristics of sport must be considered under Article 101(3) TFEU.[197]

§3. Typical Situations

I. General

443. In this section, some typical situations are evaluated in which Finnish and EU Competition rules are applied to sports events. First, the right of athletes and clubs to participate in competitions and leagues is assessed. Second, the sports federation's competence to control athletes' personal sponsor agreements is evaluated. Third, the marketing and selling of media rights to sports events are evaluated. Fourth, the transfer system of professional athletes is discussed from the point of view of EU competition law.

II. Media Rights to Sports Events

444. Today, media rights to sports events form a considerable source of income for sports associations and individual organizers and clubs. The significance of media rights has increased rapidly since the growth of pay-TV channels. Sports events are a strategic programme group by which pay-TV channels can acquire new customers and improve their market position. Sports rights can function as a tool to create an image for channels and to gain new viewers, which would otherwise be hard to reach. It has also to be remembered that media rights play a significant role in new technology. The importance of TV and other media rights has also been acknowledged in the EU which adopted the Directive 'Television Without Frontiers'.[198]

445. Questions related to the use of TV and media rights must be considered both from the seller's and buyer's perspective. A starting point is the question of the real ownership of the rights.[199] There is no common, uniform concept of ownership

197. Commission Decision 23.7.2003 Comp/C.2-37.398 – Joint selling of the commercial rights of the UEFA Champions League, paras 129–131. *See also* case T-193/02, *Laurent Piau v. the Commission*, (2005) ECR II 209, para. 105.
198. *See* Council Directive 89/552/EEC of 3 Oct. 1989 on the coordination of certain provisions laid down by Law, Regulation or Administrative Action in Member States concerning the pursuit of television broadcasting activities, OJ L 298, 17 Oct. 1989, 23–30, and Directive 2007/65/EC of the European Parliament and of the Council of 11 Dec. 2007 amending Council Directive 89/552/EEC on the coordination of certain provisions laid down by law, regulation or administrative action in Member States concerning the pursuit of television broadcasting activities, OJ L 332, 18 Dec. 2007, 27–45.
199. *See also* Pertti Lenkkeri, *Yhteiskunnallisesti merkittävien urheilutapahtumien televisiointioikeudet*, 18–22 (Turun yliopiston oikeustieteelliset tiedekunnan julkaisuja, Urheiluoikeuden sarja 20, Turku 2007).

of media rights to sports events in the EU States nor there is any definition in Community law. The question of ownership is left up to national law.

446. It has been argued in case law and in legal literature that the real organizer of a sports event owns the broadcasting rights.[200] The real organizer means the body that bears the economic risk of the event. In practice, it has been established that individual clubs, not leagues, originally own the broadcasting rights to their matches. On the contrary, in some cases, sports associations' intellectual efforts and organizational responsibility can be so important that there are sufficient grounds for establishing multiple ownership by individual clubs and sports associations. A case-by-case assessment is needed and special attention should be paid to the real efforts involved in the sports association's actions.[201]

447. From the perspective of EU competition law, it is important to recognize the conditions under which a sports association can channel broadcasting rights to itself in an agreement related to organizing rights for a sports event. These grant-back conditions might be problematic if the sports association holds a dominant market position.[202] A sports association may try to abuse its dominant market position by keeping broadcasting rights in its own possession. A sports association can, in these circumstances, try to increase its market power in the broadcasting rights market.

448. The Commission's investigation into Formula One motorsports may be mentioned as an example of a case where a sports association abused its power by placing unnecessary restrictions on promoters, circuit owners, vehicle manufacturers, and drivers.[203] The Commission held that the double role of the Fédération Internationale de l'Automobile (FIA) was problematic: the FIA was at the same time the regulator and the managing body of the commercial rights to Formula One. After negotiations between the Commission and the FIA, the double role was changed. The role of the FIA was limited to that of a sports regulator.

449. The Commission also requested some changes to the commercial agreements relating to Formula One. The length of the new free-to-air broadcasting contracts was reduced to a maximum of three years, except for contracts where specific investments justify a length of up to five years. The FIA, and some companies closely related to it, agreed to various changes in the commercial agreements on Formula One. The purpose of these changes was to lower or remove barriers to the

200. Commission Decision 23.7.2003 Comp/C.2-37.398 – Joint selling of the commercial rights of the UEFA Champions League, paras 118 and 119. *See also* Olli Rauste, *Urheiluoikeus*, 626–630 (Helsinki Lakimiesliiton Kustannus 1997).
201. Commission Decision 23.7.2003 Comp/C.2-37.398 – Joint selling of the commercial rights of the UEFA Champions League, para. 122.
202. *See also* Olli Rauste, *Urheiluoikeus*, 630–640 (Helsinki Lakimiesliiton Kustannus 1997).
203. Commission press release 30.10.2001 IP/01/1523 for closing its investigations into Formula One and other four-wheel motor sports. The Commission's investigation of the FIA regulations and commercial agreements relating to the FIA Formula One Championship came about following voluntary notifications in 1994 and 1997 requesting clearance from the European competition rules.

creation and operation of other motor vehicle series, in particular those that might compete with Formula One. The Commission closed its investigation when the above-mentioned competition problems were solved.

450. The main problems in competition law relating to TV and media rights to sports events are twofold: they involve joint selling of the rights and the exclusivity granted in broadcasting rights contracts.

A. *Joint Selling*

451. Joint selling of broadcasting rights is based on an agreement by which sports clubs assign their TV rights to the association which sells the rights on behalf of the clubs.[204] This agreement can be assessed under Article 101 TFEU. A joint selling agreement can be seen as a horizontal restriction of competition because it prevents clubs from competing in the sale of broadcasting rights. The joint selling organization reduces the number of competitors or potential competitors in the market and, therefore, it can limit competition between broadcasters. The critical factors are related to the exclusivity in premium content rights and the effects of the exercise of such rights in downstream markets.

452. Joint selling of broadcasting rights can be justified on the basis of its efficiency. Assessment of this efficiency is made by the exemption criteria set out in Article 101(3) TFEU (an improvement in production or distribution and/or promoting technical or economic progress, a fair share of the benefit to consumers, restrictions should be indispensable, no elimination of competition in respect of a substantial part of the products in question). It can be argued that joint selling improves production and distribution.

453. A single point of sale can reduce transaction costs and can help to improve the creation and maintenance of uniformity and consistency of quality. Joint selling makes it possible to create packages which would not otherwise be available. This is a question of branding. Consumers benefit from joint selling when they can buy a package which is available from a single point of sale. At the same time, it must be remembered that joint selling powers should not be unnecessarily wide. For example, the Commission decision in the UEFA case was subject to a condition which enabled football clubs to sell their live broadcasting rights to free-TV broadcasters when there is no reasonable offer from any pay-TV broadcaster.[205]

---

204. Richard Parrish & Samuli Miettinen, *The Sporting Exception in European Union Law,* 147–148 (T.M.C. Asser Press 2008). *See also* Ingrid Nitsche, *Collective Marketing of Broadcasting Rights,* 21 Eur. Competition L. Rev. 209 (2000), and Dirk Brinckman & Erik Vollebregt, *The Marketing of Sport and its Relation to E.C. Competition Law*, 19 Eur. Competition L. Rev. 284–285 (1998).
205. Commission Decision 23.7.2003 Comp/C.2-37.398 – Joint selling of the commercial rights of the UEFA Champions League, para. 168.

454. The restrictive effects of joint selling on competition greatly depend on whether complementary broadcasting rights are available in the market. If complementary broadcasting rights exist, broadcasters have different opportunities to operate and there is no fear of dependency. The way joint selling is carried out affects the possible elimination of competition. Dividing broadcasting rights into several different packages allows many media operators to acquire these rights and therefore prevents a monopoly situation from occurring on the buyers' side. Buyers have several possible sources of supply from the owners of such rights. The sale procedure is also important in this respect. Broadcasting rights should be offered for sale in a competitive bidding procedure open to all interested media operators in order to guarantee equality of opportunity among buyers.

455. The scope of the EU Competition rules also covers cooperation among broadcasting rights buyers. An important case in this respect is *Metropole télévision v. the Commission.*[206] The EGC annulled the Commission's exemption decision concerning Eurovision cooperation. According to this decision, broadcasters must obey EU competition rules, and competition restrictions cannot be solely defended on the basis of a particular public mission. However, in 2000 the Commission exempted the joint buying agreement after the European Broadcasting Union (EBU) changed its membership conditions.[207] In addition, the exemption decision was subject to a condition that required the EBU and its members to acquire broadcasting rights to sporting events only under agreements which allow the EBU and its members to give access to third parties (sub-licensing). Even this exemption decision was annulled by the EGC.[208]

B. *Exclusivity*

456. The content of TV and media rights can be assessed under Article 101 TFEU. In general, broadcasting rights are sold exclusively because this enhances the value of those rights. An agreement granting exclusive broadcasting rights can cause some competition problems. Exclusivity over a long period and for a wider range of rights can restrict competition.[209] These agreements are likely to stabilize the present market situation and lead to market foreclosure. The Commission has stated that exclusive contracts for a single sports event, or for one season in a given championship, would not normally pose any competition problems. The special characteristics of a sports event or special technical requirements for new technology have to be taken into consideration when assessing exclusive agreements. Sub-licensing can also be relevant in decision-making.

---

206. Joined Cases T-528, T-542, T-543 and T-546/93, *Métropole télévision SA and others v. the Commission*, (1996) ECR II 649.
207. Commission Decision Case IV/32.150 – *Eurovision*, 10.5.2000, OJ L 151, 24 Jun. 2000, 18–41.
208. Joined Cases T-185/00, T-216/00, T-299/00 and T-300/00, *Métropole télévision SA and others v. the Commission*, (2002) ECR II 3805.
209. *See*, e.g., Richard Parrish & Samuli Miettinen, *The Sporting Exception in European Union Law*, 146–147 (T.M.C. Asser Press 2008). *See also* Hazel Fleming, *Exclusive Rights to Broadcast Sporting Events in Europe*, 20 Eur. Competition L. Rev. 143–148 (1999).

457. The packaging of broadcasting rights can alleviate competition problems caused by exclusivity clauses. This was noted by the Commission in its decision concerning the joint selling of the commercial rights of the UEFA Champions League.[210] Packaging prevented one broadcaster from gaining all the rights when the other broadcasters dropped out of the market. At the same time, a basis for more efficient use of broadcasting rights was created: when broadcasting rights are possessed by one company, it can be assumed that some of the broadcasting rights would be unused. This would restrict economic improvement in the market.

C. Dominant Market Position

458. A seller of TV and media rights can have a dominant market position in the relevant market. A dominant market position can be based on the fact that different sports and sports events are weak substitutes.[211] The substitution is extremely weak in the case of the Olympic Games and World Championships. In these situations, the dominant seller must act in a non-discriminatory and reasonable way.

459. The counterpart of the seller's dominant market position is related to a concentration in the buyer's market. This matter has been dealt with especially in the Commission's merger decisions. Concentration in the media market decreases the number of distribution channels, which in turn affects the operating conditions for broadcasting rights sellers and broadcasters. In most cases, mergers in the media market have not been prohibited but the competitive problems have been solved by undertakings proposed by the parties. Undertakings have covered, for example, access to technical platforms[212] and the non-discriminatory treatment of competitors in broadcasting rights selling.[213]

III. Participation in Sports Events

460. Participation in a sports event is a precondition for an athlete or a sports club to receive economic benefits for their skills and resources. A professional athlete's income usually consists mainly of prize money from sports events and sponsorship agreements, whose economic value depends on success in competitions. A sports club normally obtains a major part of its income from home games (e.g., ticket sales and payments for TV rights) and sponsorship agreements, which are based on the presence of sponsors' trademarks in stadiums. The right to participate in sports events greatly affects the economic activities of a professional athlete or a sports club.

---

210. Commission Decision 23.7.2003 Comp/C.2-37.398 – Joint selling of the commercial rights of the UEFA Champions League, paras 194 and 195.
211. *See also* Jens Pelle van der Brinck, *E.C. Competition Law and the Regulation of Football: Part I*, 21(8) Eur. Competition L. Rev. 361 (2000), and Dirk Brinckman & Erik Vollebregt, *The Marketing of Sport and Its Relation to E.C. Competition Law*, 19 Eur. Competition L. Rev. 287 (1998).
212. Commission Decision 21.3.2000 Case No. Comp/Jv.37 – *B Sky B – Kirch Pay TV*, 20–26.
213. Commission Decision 7.10.1996 Case No. IV/M.779 – Bertelsmann / CLT, 9–10.

461. An organizer of a sports event can have a dominant market position as defined in Article 102 TFEU in relation to athletes. The assessment of dominance is based on the facts of each case. In legal literature, it has been stated that some sports events (the Olympic Games, World Championships and other championships, which are unique for a certain period of time) are so important for athletes that the organizers of these events hold a dominant market position.[214]

462. A dominant market position narrows the organizer's freedom of action in relation to the athletes.[215] Participation in a sports event can be seen as being based on an agreement between the organizer and the athlete. An organizer is obliged to act in a non-discriminatory and reasonable way when negotiating and enforcing this contract.

463. Non-discrimination means in practice that athletes should be chosen to participate in a competition according to conditions which have been set in advance. These conditions must not themselves be discriminatory. An organizer should not abuse their dominant market position by using participation conditions that restrict a participant's freedom of action in an excessive manner. An organizer can abuse their dominant market position by trying to strengthen their market position in other markets than the market organizing sports events. A typical case concerns the situation where an organizer excessively restricts an athlete's right to sell space for sponsor logos on his sportswear, and in so doing tries to attract new sponsorship agreements.

464. In team sports, the sports association or league, which organizes the series, can have a dominant market position in relation to the clubs.[216] The organizer normally has the right to decide which teams are entitled to participate in the series. Participation can be seen to be based on a contract which is made between the organizer and a club. If the organizer has a dominant market position, it should follow the above-mentioned requirements for non-discriminatory and reasonable behaviour.[217] The uncertainty of results is one of the leading factors when deciding which clubs have the right to participate in a league. This is a legitimate aim in the sports market. From the point of view of competition laws, it is important to ensure that new clubs are treated in a non-discriminatory way in relation to each other or to older clubs.

465. Conditions for participating in a league have close connections to the specific characteristics of sport. The Commission stated in its decision concerning UEFA Cup matches that an obligation for clubs to play their home games in their

---

214. *See* Olli Rauste, *Urheiluoikeus*, 214–218 (Helsinki Lakimiesliiton Kustannus 1997). *See also* Richard Parrish & Samuli Miettinen, *The Sporting Exception in European Union Law*, 126 (The Hague T.M.C. Asser Press 2008).
215. *See also* Olli Rauste, *Urheiluoikeus*, 223–227 (Helsinki Lakimiesliiton Kustannus 1997).
216. *See* Finnish Basketball Association and Joensuun Kataja ry, Competition Council, Dnro 7/359/96, 9 Feb. 1998, 32–35.
217. *See* Finnish Basketball Association and Joensuun Kataja ry, Competition Council, Dnro 7/359/96, 9 Feb. 1998, 34.

hometown was related purely to sporting interests.[218] The aim of this rule was to guarantee equal conditions for each club. The Commission mentioned, however, that this rule can in certain circumstances be critically evaluated under Article 102 TFEU. This approach is even more likely after the Meca-Medina judgment of the ECJ. If sporting rules affect economic activity, they basically fall under EU competition norms. The legitimate aim of a sports rule is taken into account when applying Articles 101 and 102 TFEU.

466. Conditions for participating in a league or a competition can be discussed under Article 101 TFEU.[219] In such cases, conditions for participating are assessed on the basis of a joint decision made by individual organizers or clubs. Conditions are problematic if their object is to restrict competition or if they have the effect of restricting competition for the benefit of existing organizers or clubs. The Commission defined the UEFA rule on 'Integrity of the UEFA club competitions: independence of clubs' as a decision taken by an association of associations of undertakings.[220] The Commission stated in its decision that the aim of the decision (maintenance of the public's confidence in the fairness and authenticity of the game) was legitimate. The Commission further stated that the rule did not go beyond what is necessary to ensure its legitimate aim and that the rule fell outside the scope of Article 101(1) TFEU.

467. There have been some cases in Finland in which the competences of national sports federations to control conditions for participating in a competition have been evaluated in the context of the Finnish Competition Act. These cases have concerned a national sports federation's ability to sanction sports clubs which have participated in so-called wild sports competitions (i.e., sports competitions not sanctioned by a sports federation).

468. In the first case, the Finnish Automobile Sport Federation (AKK-Motorsport) published on its website a notice in which it was stated that competitions organized by a sports club (Autokilpailuharrastajat AKH ry) were not sanctioned by AKK-Motorsport and there were serious shortcomings in the insurance coverage in these competitions.[221] It was also stated in the notice that AKK-Motorsport would sanction all the registered drivers who participated in these competitions. AKH made a complaint to the Finnish Competition and Consumer Authority. It stated that these claims were unfounded and AKK-Motorsport had abused its dominant market position by publishing the above-mentioned notice which, in practice, restricted drivers' chances to participate in different sports competitions.

218. IP/99/965, 9 Dec. 1999, IP 99/956, 9 Jun. 1999.

219. *See*, e.g., the Opinion of Advocate General Cosmas in Joined Cases C-51/96 and 191/97, *Cristelle Deliége v. Asbl Ligue Francophone de judo et disciplines associées*, (2000) ECR I 2549.

220. Case Comp/37 806: ENIC/UEFA.

221. AKK-Motosport ry, The Finnish Competition and Consumer Authority, Dnro 329/61/2003, 9 Jun. 2004.

469. The Finnish Competition and Consumer Authority stated in its decision that sports federations can, based on their position in the European Sports Model, have a decisive influence on commercial activities in the sport they are sanctioning. In these circumstances, it is essential that sports federations' decisions are transparent and non-discriminatory. In order to achieve this goal, the Finnish Competition and Consumer Authority had previously negotiated with AKK-Motorsport to change some of its regulations and by-laws.

470. The Finnish Competition and Consumer Authority stated in its previous decision that the above-mentioned changes had safeguarded possibilities for licensed drivers and other athletes to participate in sports competitions organized by associations not sanctioned by AKK-Motorsport under the condition that those competitions reached the necessary criteria for safety and technical neutrality, and fulfilled the general principles in motorsport. After the changes, the rules of AKK-Motorsport did not prevent unsanctioned undertakings to organize motorsport competitions and left reasonable opportunities for these undertakings to cooperate with AKK-Motorsport.

471. The Finnish Competition and Consumer Authority stated in its decision that there was a contradiction between the notice published on the website of AKK-Motorsport and the commitments AKK-Motorsport had given in the previous process. The Finnish Competition and Consumer Authority also negotiated with the FSF in order to eliminate the restraint of competition. After negotiations, AKK-Motorsport announced that it had removed the notice from its websites and that the state of affairs mentioned in the notice was de facto changed based on some changes in the rules of AKK-Motorsport. In these circumstances, the Finnish Competition and Consumer Authority was able to state in its decision that the restraint on competition mentioned in the complaint concerning AKH did not exist anymore in the market and, therefore, there were no legal or factual aspects which required investigating in the case. On these grounds, the Finnish Competition and Consumer Authority closed its files.

472. The second case concerned a complaint made by a motor association (Satakunta Enduro Cup ry).[222] It was claimed in the complaint that the Finnish Motor Association (SML) had abused its dominant market position by restricting its member clubs and their members opportunities to participate in motorsports competitions unsanctioned by the SML. It was further stated in the complaint that the SML had sent its member clubs and drivers, who had participated in the above-mentioned competitions, an official notice stating that they had committed an offence which would be sanctioned by an automatic withdrawal of competition licences for six months. Satakunta Enduro CUP claimed that the SML tried to prevent other sports associations from organizing motorsports competitions and this had harmful effects on the workable market conditions.

222. Suomen Moottoriliitto ry, The Finnish Competition and Consumer Authority, Dnro 903/61/2008, 8 Apr. 2014.

473. The SML stated in its response that it had controlled the legality and safety of motorsport competitions by its rules. These rules required that every motorsport competition must have prior approval of the SML. The SML further stated that it had not monitored other Finnish organizers of motorsport competitions in an active way. The above-mentioned official notice was only sent to members of the SML and their members who had participated in motorsport competitions which have failed to fulfil general safety regulations in motorsport.

474. The SML stated in response to the Finnish Competition and Consumer Authority that it had changed its rules and an automatic withdrawal of competition licences for six months was abolished. After these changes, a withdrawal of competition licences has always been based on concrete facts concerning participating in a motorsport competition both unsanctioned by the SML and organized in an illegal way. Such decisions can be brought before the Finnish Sports Arbitration Board. The SML also claimed that it did not have these disciplinary decisions in practice.

475. The Finnish Competition and Consumer Authority stated in its decision that economic activities related to sport can be evaluated based on the Finnish Competition Act. However, this case did not concern a restraint of competition but had harmful effects on workable market conditions mentioned in section 1 of the Act. The Finnish Competition Authority has a duty to investigate restraints of competition only if these restraints are relevant in the context of the national economy. The economic activities in this case were limited by their scope and there was no need, related to general interest, to investigate these possible restrictions. Therefore, the Finnish Competition and Consumer Authority decided not to investigate the case in detail and closed its files. It is worth noticing that the decision made by the Finnish Competition and Consumer Authority does not contain a material evaluation of the case. The Finnish Competition and Consumer Authority can reopen its investigations if new information is presented concerning the harmful effects of the arrangement.

476. The Finnish case law can be seen as underdeveloped concerning national sports federations' competence to regulate conditions for their members participating in different sports competitions and abuse of dominant market positions. The crucial questions related to the Finnish Competition Act have not been evaluated materially. The two cases elaborated on here concerned the Finnish Competition and Consumer Authority's competence to prioritize its tasks. Unfortunately, material evaluations of these questions by the Market Court or the Supreme Administrative Court (KHO) are still lacking in Finland.

477. It is interesting to notice that the strategic line followed by the Finnish Competition and Consumer Authority seems to differ from that in Sweden and in EU.[223] The Swedish Market Court found that a sports federation may refuse its members the right to participate in the competitions of competing organizations

223. Case A 5/11, *Svenska Bilsportförbundet v. Konkurrensverket*, The Swedish Market Court, 20 Dec. 2012; Case T–93/18, *International Skating Union v. European Commission*, ECLI:EU:T:2020:610.

when this would make it impossible to safely conduct the other competition, sanctioned by this sports federation, taking place at the same time.[224] The rules, which constituted an absolute ban, were disproportionally restrictive for the purpose of achieving this objective. The General Court of European Union (EGC) considered the International Skating Union's (ISU's) eligibility rules under Article 101 TFEU. The ISU had very comprehensive eligibility rules preventing speed skaters from participating in any speed skating events not sanctioned by the ISU or one of its members. The EGC stated that the eligibility rules had as their object the restriction of competition within the meaning of Article 101(1) TFEU when taking into consideration their content, objectives and the legal and economic context. The EGJ also discussed in its decision whether the effect of the eligibility rules was a restriction of competition. The eligibility rules resulted in an output restriction when the organization of new, unsanctioned speed skating events was prevented. Simultaneously, consumer choice and innovation were diminished because unsanctioned organizers could not provide innovative formats of speed skating events for consumers.

IV. Athlete's Personal Sponsorship Agreements

478. There have been some cases in Finland where the relationship between the sponsorship agreements of a sports federation and those of an athlete has been evaluated in the context of competition law. The key question concerns whether a sports federation can control or restrict sponsors with whom an athlete can have cooperation or whether this constitutes an abuse of dominant market position. In practice, this question is relevant because these sponsors can be active in the same market or even be competitors. It has been common practice to have a clause in an agreement between a sports federation and an athlete which restricts the athletes' freedom to sign sponsorship agreements in these cases.

479. The first and most well-known case concerned an athlete agreement which was made between the Finnish Ski Federation and the ski jumpers Matti Hautamäki and Jussi Hautamäki.[225] These athletes made a complaint to Finnish Competition and Consumer Authority and asked whether the Finnish Ski Federation had abused its dominant market position when it had prevented their right to engage in commercial activity based on contractual disagreements.

480. The athletes claimed that the Finnish Ski Federation held a dominant market position in ski sports in Finland. This de facto monopoly position was based on the rules of the International Ski Federation (Federation Internationale de Ski, FIS). The Finnish Ski Federation was a *partenaire obligatoire* if an individual wanted to be a professional athlete in ski sports in Finland. Only the Finnish Ski Federation

224. *See also* Johan Lindholm, *The Impact of SBF v. KKV on Sport: Swedish Fender-Bender or European Pileup?*, 34 Eur. Competition L. Rev. 367–372 (2013).

225. The Finnish Competition and Consumer Authority, 756/61/04, 11 Nov. 2004.

could offer coaching services related to ski jumping on a professional level in Finland and had the sole competence to assign ski jumpers to international competitions organized by the FIS.

481. On a regular basis, the Finnish Ski Federation entered into contracts with ski jumpers in the national team. These contracts covered, among other things, the terms for the division of commercial rights between the parties. Based on this contract, the ski jumper had the right to have their sponsors' logos on the skies. The athletes in this case then made sponsor agreements with a German car manufacturer, a German brewery, and an English betting company. The Finnish Ski Federation refused to accept these sponsors because they were operating in the same market as the sponsors of the federation. According to the agreement made between the athletes and the Finnish Ski Federation, the athletes had no right to make sponsorship agreements with sponsors operating in the same market as the sponsors of the federation. The Finnish Ski Federation threatened to ban the athletes from the national team if they tried to participate in sports competitions with other than officially approved sponsor logos on their skies.

482. The Finnish Competition and Consumer Authority stated in its decision that the athletes who made the complaint could be evaluated as undertakings mentioned in the Finnish Competition Act because they engaged in commercial activities. Additionally, it was stated in the decision that the Finnish Ski Federation had a dominant market position in the relevant market. A dominant undertaking has a special responsibility not to harm workable market conditions when making contractual arrangements. In practice, the dominant undertaking's freedom of contract can be restricted in certain cases in order to safeguard workable market conditions. A dominant undertaking, for example, may not apply dissimilar conditions to equivalent transactions with trading partners, thereby placing them at a competitive disadvantage.

483. The athletes argued in the case that the practice imposed by the Finnish Ski Federation, in fact, had harmful effects on the sponsor market. However, the Finnish Competition and Consumer Authority stated that there were several options for possible sponsors to make cooperation and sponsorship agreements. There were many relevant alternatives in sport but also in other fields of activities. Therefore, the option provided by the Finnish Ski Federation was not unique. On the contrary, a potential sponsor could have publicity for its brand and products, for example, via television, the internet, and trade fairs. The Finnish Competition and Consumer Authority also stated that potential sponsors were typically international corporations who were not dependent on the Finnish Ski Federation and the services provided by it.

484. The Finnish Competition and Consumer Authority also evaluated the case from the perspective of the athletes. It stated that the athletes had plenty of opportunities to make sponsorship agreements even though there was the abovementioned clause in the athlete's agreement. The clause was based on a long contractual usage which is linked to the relevant interests of the partners of the Finnish Ski Federation. The clause also prevented so-called free riding which had harmful effects on dynamic efficiency. Abolishing the clause might lead to consequences which could be fatal to the fundraising system of the Finnish Ski Federation. The Finnish Competition and Consumer Authority stated in its decision that competition in the relevant might be considered functional as a whole, irrespective of the suspected infringement. In these circumstances, there was no need for further investigations.

485. An appeal against the decision of the Finnish Competition and Consumer Authority was made by a company representing the athletes in the sphere of commercial agreements.[226] The Market Court ruled that the appeal was inadmissible because the company did not have a legitimate interest in the case, required by the Administrative Judicial Procedure Act (586/96). The decision of the Finnish Competition and Consumer Authority was not directed at the company and it only had indirect effects on the legal status of the company.

486. After the *Hautamäki* case, the question of whether a sports federation can control or restrict sponsors with whom an athlete can have cooperation or whether this constitutes an abuse of dominant market position has been evaluated in at least one other case.[227] The case concerned a Finnish athlete who had a sponsorship agreement with a German cartridge manufacturer. The Finnish Shooting Sport Federation had, for its part, a sponsorship agreement with a Finnish cartridge manufacturer. The Finnish Shooting Sport Federation made an athlete agreement with all members of the national team; signing this contract was a precondition for membership in the national team and assignment to international competitions.

487. The division of commercial rights between the Finnish Shooting Sport Federation and the athletes was made in the agreement. There was a clause in the agreement which forbade sponsor logos of those undertakings competing on the same market with the Finnish Shooting Sport Federations sponsors in athlete's sports equipment in international competitions. The athlete claimed that the Finnish Shooting Sport Federation had a dominant market position and it had abused this position by requiring him to sign the above-mentioned agreement. In practice, the agreement restricted the athlete's freedom to have sponsors and had adverse effects on workable market conditions. Based on these and numerous other claims, the athlete made a complaint to the Finnish Competition and Consumer Authority.

488. The Finnish Competition and Consumer Authority did not investigate the complaint.[228] The Finnish Competition and Consumer Authority referred to the above-mentioned *Hautamäki* case and stated that competition in the relevant market might be considered functional as a whole, irrespective of the suspected infringement. The Finnish Competition and Consumer Authority also stated that the

226. The Market Court, MAO:215/06, 11 Oct. 2006.
227. The Market Court, MAO:244/13, 5 Jun. 2013.
228. The Finnish Competition and Consumer Authority, 407/14.00.00/2010, 21 Jun. 2012.

case was more concerned with the contractual relationship between the athlete and the Finnish Shooting Sport Federation and it is not a task of the Authority to decide these questions. The athlete made an appeal against this decision. The Market Court dismissed the appeal and stated that the Finnish Competition and Consumer Authority had a right not to investigate the case. This decision was challenged by the athlete. The KHO dismissed the appeal by its decision on 16 September 2015.[229]

V. Transfer Rules

489. The relationship between the transfer rules for professional players and Articles 101 and 102 TFEU has been discussed in detail in the Opinion of the Advocate General Lenz in the *Bosman* case.[230] The ECJ did not consider this relationship in its own judgment.

490. Transfer rules can be seen as a cartel infringing Article 101 TFEU. The transfer system is based on agreements between individual clubs or a decision of an association of undertakings. Transfer rules can artificially restrict supply and demand in the player market. Transfer rules form a mechanism by which the existing competition situation can be preserved in the market.

491. Advocate General Lenz concluded that the transfer system in the *Bosman* case was a cartel infringing Article 101 TFEU. However, Advocate General Lenz further concluded that the transfer system cannot be seen as an abuse within the meaning of Article 102 TFEU. According to Lenz, the transfer rules did not concern the power in the market that the clubs taken together had over competitors, customers, or consumers. The transfer system concerned only the relationship between the clubs and players which, in Lenz's opinion, differs from the relationship between clubs and competitors, and customers and consumers.

492. After the Bosman decision, there has been a significant change from the transfer fee system to the training compensation system.[231] The present system can be said to have some legitimate objectives (e.g., the education of young players).[232] New fees cannot just be a replacement for the old system. Therefore, the proper level of fees is important. In addition, the age limits adopted in the new systems may be mentioned.

229. The Supreme Administrative Court, 2445, 2146/3/13, 16 Sep. 2015.
230. *See*, e.g., Opinion of Advocate General Lenz in case C-415/93, *Union royale belge des societes de football association ASBL v. Bosman*, ECR 1995 I 4921, para. 255.
231. *See*, e.g., Richard Parrish & Samuli Miettinen, *The Sporting Exception in European Union Law*, 175–178 (The Hague T.M.C. Asser Press 2008). *See also* generally Esa Schön, *Työntekijöiden vapaan liikkuvuuden periaate ja joukkueurheilu*, 55–59 (Opetusministeriö, Kulttuuri-, liikunta- ja nuorisopolitiikan osaston julkaisusarja 4/2002, Helsinki 2002).
232. *See also* Johanna Lahti, *UEFA's Homegrown Player Rule in the Light of EU Law*, 38–42 (Turun yliopiston oikeustieteellisen tiedekunnan julkaisuja, Urheiluoikeuden sarja 29, Turku 2010).

493. Abolition of the old transfer rules has not led to totally free player transfers. These transfers can be restricted for reasons related to the specific characteristics of sport. According to the principle established in the *Lehtonen* case, it is possible to impose time limits in order to prevent artificial changes in team rosters before playoff games.[233] Time limits can be justified for reasons which relate to the specific characteristics of sport and they do not, in principle, cause competition problems. The actual definition of time limits is obviously a separate question.

494. There are additional restrictions on player agreements and player transfers in some sports (such as football). These restrictions are set by the sports associations' own decisions. Restrictions can cover, for example, the minimum and maximum duration of contracts and unilateral breaches of contracts. The Commission accepted the transfer rules adopted in football,[234] but despite the Commission's approval, some critical observations may be made.[235] These critical observations concern, for example, the role that the specific characteristics of sport can legitimately have in the application of Articles 101 and 102 TFEU. Strong arguments can be presented for and against the decision made by the Commission. These questions remain open until a judgment by the ECJ or the EGC is available.

§4. Conclusion

495. Case law provides solid principles for applying Finnish and EU competition rules to sports activities. The practice of sport is subject to EU competition law only so far as it constitutes an economic activity within the meaning of Article 2 of the EC Treaty. EU competition law is not applied in a vacuum. The specific characteristics of sport can and must be taken into consideration when applying Articles 101(1), 101(3) and 102 TFEU. However, the fact should be recognized that the structure of EU competition norms and its case law form a framework within which the specific characteristics of sport can have relevance. In the future, it will be more or less a question of defining the content of this framework. Despite present case law, many important questions on the interface between competition law and sport still remain unanswered. It is the duty of the courts of law, competition authorities, as well as researchers, to answer these questions.

233. Case C-176/96, *Lehtonen and Castors Canada Dry Namur-Braine v. Fédération royale belge des sociétés de Basketball et Asbl Basket Liga-ligue Basket Belgium*, (2000) ECR I 2681.

234. Commission press release IP /02/824 5.6.2002 for closing investigations into FIFA regulations on international football transfers.

235. *See* e.g., Stephen Weatherill, *'Fair Play Please!': Recent Developments in the Application of EC Law to Sport*, 40 Com. Mkt. Rev., 70–72 (2003).

Chapter 2. Commercial Contracts in Sport

§1. Introduction

496. Contract law creates legal preconditions for cooperation between individuals and for economic exchange. Various commercial contracts are made in sport. In many cases, the special features of sport are not directly relevant when evaluating these contracts from a legal perspective (e.g., lease contracts for sports facilities). However, some characteristics of commercial contracts dealing with sport can be defined. These contracts are made between parties of which, at least one is a sports organization or an athlete. Additionally, these contracts concern different sporting activities, thus it is important to know the relevant context of sport when applying them. Commercial contracts in sport can have different forms and contents (individually negotiated contracts, standard contracts, business-to-business contracts, consumer contracts, arm's-length contracts or long-term contracts) which increases the challenges to evaluating these contracts systemically.

497. There is no special legislation in Finland concerning commercial agreements in sport. However, some exceptions exist. In the case of a player's contract, the Finnish Employment Contracts Act (55/2001) is applicable. This legal background has some consequences. First, the general principles of contract law are relevant when evaluating commercial agreements in sport. Contract law has four general legal principles (the will principle, the reliance principle, the conscionability principle, and the protection of the weaker party principle).[236] Second, general legislation concerning contracts can also be applied in these cases. This legislation forms a solid basis for legal evaluation of commercial contracts in sport. The Contracts Act (228/1929) is a central part of the relevant legislation in this respect.

498. The Contracts Act covers various aspects of contract law which are also relevant when evaluating commercial agreements in sport. Crucial issues concern, for example, conclusion of contracts, authorization, and adjustments of contracts. Section 1 of the Contracts Act states that an offer to conclude a contract and the acceptance of such an offer should bind the offeror and the acceptor, as provided in the second chapter of the Contracts Act. There are various sections in Chapter 1 of the Contracts Act which are also relevant in this respect.[237] The basic legal requirements for authorization are defined in Chapter 2 of the Contracts Act.[238] They are also applicable in cases of commercial contracts in sport.

---

236. *See* Antti Aine, *Kilpailu ja sopimus*, 151–154 (Helsinki Suomalainen Lakimiesyhdistys 2011).
237. Only some of them can be referred to here. According to s. 2, if the offeror has fixed a specified period of time for acceptance, he or she must be deemed to have stipulated that the acceptance has to reach him or her within the said period of time. According to s. 3, an offer made orally without granting respite for acceptance must be accepted immediately; unless an immediate acceptance is given, the offer must be deemed rejected. According to s. 4, an acceptance that reaches the offeror too late must be deemed to constitute a new offer made by the original acceptor.
238. According to s. 10 of the Contracts Act, a person who has authorized another to conclude contracts or to enter into other transactions must, directly in relation to a third person, acquire rights and become bound by way of the transactions entered into by the agent within the scope of his or her

499. Commercial contracts can be seen as mechanisms for cooperation between parties. The balance of interests is important for any commercial relationship to function well. However, practical matters and events can disturb the above-mentioned balance. Therefore, it is important to have legal mechanisms for the adjustment of contracts. In the Finnish legal system, Chapter 3 of the Contracts Act provides legal tools for the adjustments of contracts. According to section 36 of the Contracts Act, a contract term which is unfair or whose application would lead to an unfair result may be adjusted or set aside. In determining what is unfair, regard has to be given to the entire contents of the contract, the positions of the parties, the circumstances prevailing at and after the conclusion of the contract, and other factors. If a term referred to is such that it would be unfair to enforce the rest of the contract after the adjustment of the term, the rest of the contract may also be adjusted or declared terminated. A provision relating to the amount of consideration that must be given is also to be deemed a contract term.

500. Occasionally, standard contracts are used in sport. In these cases, the relevant doctrine and case law in Finland concerning standard contracts has to be taken into consideration. Unfortunately, it is evident that the case law related to commercial standard contracts in sport is very limited. It has also to be remembered that standard contract clauses can be replaced by individually negotiated terms. This part of the current legal status of commercial agreements is unsatisfactory and provides challenges for sports federations, sports clubs, and athletes to govern in advance risks related to these contracts.

501. Legal discussions on commercial contracts in sport have been, at least so far, limited in Finland.[239] Employment contracts and sponsorship agreements have been the few exceptions in this respect. In the following chapter, sponsorship agreements will be evaluated as a Finnish example of commercial contracts in sport. In this way, it is possible to discuss, from the Finnish perspective, the relevance of the context of sport when applying contract law.

---

authority and in the name of the principal. Where a person, by virtue of employment or otherwise by way of a contract concluded with another, holds a position which, according to law or custom, establishes a certain authority to act on behalf of the other, he or she must be deemed, within the scope of that authority, empowered to conclude contracts or to enter into other transactions. According to s. 11 of the Contracts Act, where an agent has entered into a transaction against the instructions of the principal, the transaction should not bind the principal if the third person knew or should have known that the agent was exceeding the scope of his or her authority. Where an authorization is based solely on a communication by the principal to the agent, transactions by the agent exceeding the scope of his or her authority should not bind the principal even if the third person was in good faith. Additionally, it is stated in s. 12 of the Contracts Act that an authorization expressly communicated by the principal to a third person must be revoked when an express communication by the principal revoking the authorization reaches the third person.

239. *See* Olli Rauste, *Urheiluoikeus*, 43–63 (Helsinki Lakimiesliiton Kustannus 1997). *See also* Noora Jokela, *Urheilusponsorin intressien turvaaminen sopimuskumppanin julkisuuskuvan muuttuessa* (Opetusministeriö, Kulttuuri-, liikunta- ja nuorisopolitiikan osaston julkaisusarja 13/2000, Helsinki 2000), and Kati Rinne, *Yksilöurheilijan vahingonkorvausvastuu sponsorisopimusketjussa* (Turun yliopiston oikeustieteellisen tiedekunnan julkaisuja, Urheiluoikeuden sarja 28, Turku 2010).

§2. Sponsorship Agreements

502. Sponsorship agreements have become common in Finland, which can be seen as a part of the commercialization of sport. They can be defined in sport as a typical contract that is combined by different aspects.[240] There is no special legislation on sponsorship agreements in Finland. Therefore, the content and legal status of sponsorships agreements should be evaluated based on relevant case law and contractual practices.

503. The importance of sponsorship agreements has been noticed by sports federations in Finland. By 2004, the FSF had already nominated a working group to prepare a report concerning sponsorship agreements. The working group consisted of both legal experts and representatives of FSFs and sports leagues. In its report, the working group considered sponsorship agreements from various perspectives.[241] The report has had a significant influence when evaluating sponsorship agreements in Finland. This situation has partly been necessary because of the fact that the national legal discussion on sponsorship agreements has so far been limited in its scope.[242]

504. Sponsorship agreements can be seen to cover a wide range of different commercial arrangements. They can be made with sponsors by sports federations, sports clubs, or athletes. A typical feature of sponsorship agreements is their cooperative nature. From the perspective of a sponsor, the goals of the contractual arrangement do not only concern financially supporting an athlete, a sports club, or a sports federation. On the contrary, a sponsor has, at least in most cases, legitimate expectations concerning the mutual gains of a contractual relationship. Cooperation can involve, for example, licensing an intellectual property right or providing other valuable services. This dimension of sponsorship agreements has become increasingly important during the 2000s.

505. In principle, the parties can stipulate the content of a sponsorship agreement as they wish. This competence is based on the freedom of contract provisions guaranteed in section 15 of the Constitution of Finland. Contractual clauses can be defined in different ways. A common feature of most sponsorship agreements is to promote a sponsor's brand via sport and gain positive publicity for the brand. A sponsorship agreement provides a good tool to achieve these goals. In addition, various risks can be linked to a sponsorship agreement. These risks often concern changes in the public image of an athlete, a sports club or a sports federation. In practice, one of the highest risks can be realized in doping cases. Cooperating with an athlete or a sports club in the middle of a doping case is not always a positive thing for a sponsor and its business image.

---

240. *See also* Heikki Halila, *Urheilusopimukset*, 294–298 (in Heikki Halila & Mika Hemmo (eds), Sopimustyypit (2nd ed., Helsinki Talentum 2008)).
241. Sponsorisopimustyöryhmän mietintö (Helsinki the Finnish Sports Federation 2006).
242. *See* generally Olli Rauste, *Urheiluoikeus*, 43–69 (Helsinki Lakimiesliiton Kustannus 1997).

506. A key thing when preparing a sponsorship agreement is to govern in advance the possible risks related to a contractual relationship. From the legal perspective, this is possible by using specified contractual clauses. These clauses make sure that a sponsorship agreement can reach the goals set by the parties. In practice, these terms can concern cancellation of an agreement and liquidated damages. It is also essential that the mutual goals of an arrangement are properly defined in an agreement. These clauses (e.g., whereas clauses) have relevance when applying for a sponsorship agreement. At the same time, they also enhance the importance of general commercial practices as a basis for interpretation. The importance of this perspective has been emphasized in legal discussions concerning sponsorship agreements in Finland.[243]

507. Typically, sponsorship relationships are by their nature long-term arrangements. This temporal dimension of sponsorship agreements raises the question of how to govern changing circumstances. Not all the risks related to the temporal dimension of a sponsorship agreement are necessarily unpredictable. They do not cause a legitimate reason to cancel a sponsorship agreement unless otherwise agreed. One example of such risks that can be mentioned is the fact that an athlete or a sports club has gained less success in sports competitions than expected in advance. However, there can also be various other legitimate reasons to cancel a sponsorship agreement. When an athlete ends his or her professional career, there are, in principle, no legal grounds to require a sponsor not to cancel a sponsorship agreement. The same conclusion can even be reached when an athlete is injured and is unable to fulfil most of his or her obligations based on a sponsorship agreement for a considerable period of time.

508. A sponsorship agreement often covers marketing or promoting a product or a service in sport. In these cases, the legality of the marketing measures has to be evaluated. Marketing a product or a service is governed in Finland by, for example, the Consumer Protection Act (38/1978) and the Unfair Business Practices Act (1061/1978). A special interest in the Finnish sports system has been concerned with the marketing of lotto games, betting games, instant games, and other games, which involve a draw. From the legal perspective, the Finnish gaming operators have a monopoly guaranteed in the Finnish legislation. Therefore, there are some wide restrictions on the marketing operations of other gaming operators in Finland.[244] This background has to be taken into consideration when preparing sponsorship agreements in Finland.

509. In the context of self-governance in sport, there have been some discussions in Finland concerning the competence of sports federations to restrict their member clubs' freedom to engage in commercial cooperation with other than Finnish gaming operators. This competence has been seen justified because one of the Finnish gaming operators (Veikkaus) has contributed its total proceeds to the Finnish Ministry of Education and Culture which has distributed them further to Finnish

243. Sponsorisopimustyöryhmän mietintö, 40–41 (Helsinki the Finnish Sports Federation 2006).
244. *See also* Decision of the Supreme Court KKO 2005:27.

arts, sports, science, and youth work.[245] However, it should be noticed that this question has not yet been realized because the marketing operations of foreign gaming operators are forbidden based on the Finnish legislation. It is worth noticing that national gambling legislation is under revision in Finland. The Finnish gaming operators' monopoly guaranteed in the legislation will be abolished, and there will be a licence system for gaming operators. The revision will take place at the very latest on 1 January 2026. After the revision, any gambling directed at the Finnish market without a Finnish licence will be illegal and it will be also prohibited to market or advertise such gambling.

510. Sponsorship agreements cover in most cases a transfer of intellectual property rights. These rights can be transferred directly from the original holder of these rights to a sponsor or indirectly to a sponsor who can use these rights in its commercial operations. Rights conferred to a sponsor are often exclusive in order to maximize their value to a sponsor. In practice, sponsorship agreements can, for example, concern the right to use a name of an athlete, a sports club or a sports federation in marketing. In some cases, a sponsor acquires a right to use a picture of an athlete or a team in marketing.

511. From the legal perspective, it is interesting to evaluate how the transfer of these rights can be constructed. In a relationship between a player and a sports club, a player can transfer his right to a club as a part of a player agreement. In principle, there are no legal reasons to see this transfer as being unjustified. A player receives compensation for this transfer as a part of a player agreement. In exceptional cases, the contract term can be seen as unfair and, based on section 36 of the Contracts Act (228/1929), the term may be adjusted or set aside. In determining what is unfair, regard has to be paid to the entire contents of the contract, the positions of the parties, the circumstances prevailing at and after the conclusion of the contract, and other factors. If a term referred to is such that it would be unfair to enforce the rest of the contract after the adjustment of the term, the rest of the contract may also be adjusted or declared terminated.

512. The question of transfer of intellectual property rights is also relevant between a sports club and a sports federation. In most cases, it is a question of TV rights and other rights relating to a sports event. These are often transferred as part of a shareholder agreement in sports leagues or in other contractual arrangements between a sports club and a sports federation. These arrangements should not only be evaluated in the context of contract law. From the perspective of EU competition law, it is important to recognize the conditions under which a sports federation can channel TV rights or other intellectual property rights to itself in an agreement related to the organizing rights for a sports event. These grant-back conditions might be problematic if the sports federation holds a dominant market position. A sports federation may try to abuse its dominant market position by keeping the TV rights in its own possession. A sports federation can in these circumstances tries to increase its market power in the TV rights market.

245. Sponsorisopimustyöryhmän mietintö, 18–20 (Helsinki the Finnish Sports Federation 2006).

513. A sports federation might have a need to control those conditions under which a sports club or an athlete can sign a sponsorship agreement. A basic distinction can be made between sport-related reasons and other, for example, commercial, reasons. There have been some discussions taking place in Finland on the competence of sports federations to restrict by their rules the opportunities of their member associations and athletes to sign sponsorship agreements which contradict the basic values of sport.[246] The discussion has been especially concerned with the marketing of alcohol products (in practice, beers) in sport. This marketing is not free in Finland. On the contrary, it is strictly governed by Finnish legislation.[247]

514. In practice, sponsorship agreements made within these legal requirements with breweries are a source of enormous income for various FSF and sports clubs. Therefore, this question has been a sensitive issue among sports federations and sports clubs in Finland. The expert group nominated by the FSF to investigate the matter came to a general conclusion in its report.[248] The expert group stated that sports federations should have the right, in principle, to govern their member association's and individual athletes' competence to formulate sponsorship agreements with breweries and other equivalent manufacturers. However, it is evident that there is no consensus about this among sports federations and other commercial actors in Finland. This situation is being closely followed by the commercial interests involved in the matter.

515. Despite the above-mentioned background, FSF are not free to govern these sponsorship agreements by their internal rules. On the contrary, the competition law perspective cannot be ignored. The internal rules of sports federations may restrict

246. Sponsorisopimustyöryhmän mietintö, 43–44 (Helsinki the Finnish Sports Federation 2006).
247. According to s. 50 of the Alcohol Act (1102/2017), it is prohibited to advertise strong alcoholic beverages. Advertising mild alcoholic beverages and linking it to advertising or sales promotion of another product or service is prohibited, for example, if:

- it is aimed at minors or other individuals to whom according to s. 37 no alcoholic beverages may be sold, or if such individuals are depicted in it;
- it is carried out in television operations between 7 p.m. and 22 p.m. or in accordance with the Act on the Classification of Audiovisual Programmes (775/2000) in connection with public presentation of an audiovisual programme allowed to persons under 18 years of age in a cinema (11.5.2007/588);
- consumption of alcohol is linked to driving a vehicle;
- the alcohol content of an alcoholic beverage is emphasized as a positive quality;
- an abundant consumption of alcohol is described in positive terms, or temperance or moderate consumption of alcohol in negative terms;
- it gives an idea that alcohol increases the functional capacity or makes one socially or sexually more successful;
- it gives an idea that alcohol has medical or therapeutic properties or that is refreshes, calms or is a means to settle conflicts; and if
- it is contrary to good manners, it uses methods that are inappropriate from the viewpoint of the consumer or otherwise gives untruthful or misleading information about alcohol, its use, effects or other properties.

248. Sponsorisopimustyöryhmän mietintö, 43–44 (Helsinki the Finnish Sports Federation 2006).

the freedom of sports clubs and breweries to engage in commercial activities. A sports federation can abuse its dominant market position if its rules are not necessary for the attainment of a justified goal.

516. The competition law perspective can also be relevant in conjunction with other aspects of sponsorship agreements. A sports federation's dominant market position is based on the pyramid structure of sport in Europe.[249] The European Sports Model opens up a de facto competence for a national sports federation to restrict athletes' opportunities to sign sponsorship agreements. In most cases, these restrictions are related to agreements on national teams and coaching services made between a sports federation and an athlete.

517. The key question concerns whether a sports federation can control or restrict the choice of sponsors with whom an athlete can cooperate or whether this constitutes an abuse of a dominant market position. In practice, this question is relevant because the sponsors can be active on the same market or be even competitors of the sponsors of the sports federation. It has been common practice that there is a clause in an agreement between a sports federation and an athlete that restricts the athletes' freedom to sign sponsorship agreements in these cases.

518. The first and most well-known case concerned an athlete agreement made between the Finnish Ski Federation and ski jumpers Matti Hautamäki and Jussi Hautamäki.[250] According to the agreement made between the athletes and the Finnish Ski Federation, the athletes had no right to make sponsorship agreements with sponsors operating in the same market as sponsors of the federation. The athletes made a complaint to Finnish Competition and Consumer Authority stating that the Finnish Ski Federation had abused its dominant market position when it had prevented their right to engage in commercial activity based on contractual disagreements.

519. The Finnish Competition and Consumer Authority stated in its decision that the athletes who made the complaint could be evaluated as undertakings mentioned in the Finnish Competition Act because they engaged in commercial activities and the Finnish Ski Federation had a dominant market position in the relevant market. The Finnish Competition and Consumer Authority further stated that there were several options of possible sponsors with whom the athletes could cooperate and make sponsorship agreements. There were many relevant alternatives in sport and also in other fields of activities. Therefore, the option provided by the Finnish Ski Federation was not unique. On the contrary, a potential sponsor could have publicity for its brand and products, for example, via television, the internet, and trade fairs. The Finnish Competition and Consumer Authority also stated that potential sponsors were typically international corporations who were not dependent on the Finnish Ski Federation and the services it provides.

249. *See also* Lars Halgreen, *European Sports Law. A Comparative Analysis of the European and American Models of Sport,* 64–65 (Kobenhavn Forlaget Thomson 2004).
250. The Finnish Competition and Consumer Authority, Decision 11.11.2004, Dnro 756/61/04.

520. The Finnish Competition and Consumer Authority also investigated the case from the perspective of the athletes. It stated that the athletes had a considerable number of opportunities to formulate sponsorship agreements despite the above-mentioned clause in the athlete's agreement. The clause was based on a long contractual usage linked to the relevant interests of the partners of the Finnish Ski Federation. The clause also prevented any so-called free riding which would have harmful effects on dynamic efficiency. Abolishing the clause might lead to consequences which could be detrimental to the fundraising system of the Finnish Ski Federation. The Finnish Competition and Consumer Authority stated in its decision that competition in the relevant market might be considered functional as a whole, irrespective of the suspected infringement. In these circumstances, there was no need for further investigations.

521. The above-mentioned decision was taken into consideration when the expert group prepared its report on sponsorship agreements.[251] The expert group stated that sports federations have a legitimate interest to safeguard commercial aspects related to their sponsorship agreements. Therefore, they can impose restrictions on individual athletes and sports clubs in cases where the sponsors in question are active in the same market or are competitors. However, a comprehensive ban is not justified. On the contrary, only reasonable and necessary restrictions can be used. Otherwise, competition law norms and sanctions might be applicable.

251. Sponsorisopimustyöryhmän mietintö, 33–35 (Helsinki the Finnish Sports Federation 2006).

Part V. COVID-2019

§1. General

522. The COVID-19 pandemic has had very wide and multidimensional effects in Finland. There are, as reported on 20 May 2021, a total of 90,946 reported cases, and the cumulative number of reported deaths associated with the disease is 929. Public authorities have decided on various restrictions to protect the lives and health of all people in Finland. These restrictions have had far-reaching effects on sports federations, sports leagues, sports clubs, athletes and other individuals.

523. Exceptional measures were needed to slow down the spreading of the coronavirus and to protect risk groups in Finland. Provisions on the powers of authorities in emergency conditions are defined in the Emergency Powers Act (1552/2011). For the first time since World War II, a state of emergency was declared in Finland. First, the Government, in cooperation with the President of the Republic, declared a state of emergency on 16 March 2020. Subsequently, on 15 June 2020, the Government announced that the situation in Finland no longer constituted a state of emergency as referred to in section 3 of the Emergency Powers Act. However, the Government then declared in its plenary session on 1 March 2021 that Finland was again in a state of emergency as referred to in section 3, paragraph 5 of the Emergency Powers Act. Finally, on 27 April 2021, the Government issued in its plenary session a decree repealing the use of powers under the Emergency Powers Act and announced that the use of these powers would end on the same day.

524. Heavy restrictions can be issued based on the Emergency Powers Act, for example, the Government's decision to restrict traffic between the region of Uusimaa and other regions on 25 March 2020. The aim of the restrictions was to prevent further coronavirus infections and to slow down the spread of the epidemic from Uusimaa to other regions of Finland. However, the powers defined in the Emergency Powers Act can only be exercised if authorities cannot control a situation with their normal powers. The COVID-19 epidemic has been managed, as far as possible, by using the standard powers of the authorities. The Communicable Diseases Act (1227/2016) has formed the most important legal basis for the authorities. The Finnish Parliament has also approved some temporary amendments to the Communicable Diseases Act and other legislation.

§2. Restrictions and Other Operations

525. The restrictions imposed following the COVID-19 pandemic must have a valid legal basis. The proportionality principle forms a solid legal structure for this discretion. The restrictions should have a justified cause, which is closely linked to the aim of protecting people's lives and health. The restrictions should also be necessary to realize a justified aim. In practice, this means that realistically there is no other way to achieve this aim. Additionally, the restriction should be proportionate.

526. The proportionality principle leads to a balancing of the different legitimate interests of various entities when imposing the above-mentioned restrictions. On the one hand, it is necessary to take into account the impact on the epidemiological situation, the economy and people's well-being. On the other hand, basic freedoms guaranteed by the Finnish Constitution and international human rights conventions are highly relevant. The task has transpired to be challenging for the politicians, the Government and the Constitutional Law Committee (Parliament of Finland).

527. Only proportionate restrictions can be implemented. As a general rule, the extent of the restrictions in place will depend on the severity of the COVID-19 situation in each region. Most regional authorities have decided on recommendations and restrictions in line with the legislation on communicable diseases (the Communicable Diseases Act). This division of powers is, in principle, legally justified, but it has also caused problems due to inconsistent decisions when implementing the restrictions.

528. The public authorities have a mandate to introduce regional restrictions on events and on business and leisure activities when this is necessary to prevent the spread of the epidemic. The restrictions may apply, for example, to the use of premises or the number of participants in activities. The Government decided on additional measures to address the coronavirus outbreak in Finland on 16 March 2020. All national and municipal hobby and leisure centres, swimming pools and other sports facilities were closed. Private and third-sector operators were advised to close their facilities. The Government and the authorities with jurisdiction implemented the above-mentioned decisions and recommendations based on the Emergency Powers Act, the Communicable Diseases Act and other legislations. Public gatherings were limited to no more than ten persons, and avoiding spending unnecessary time in public places was recommended. These decisions and recommendations prevented de facto all sporting activities in Finland.[252] All the major sports leagues were forced to stop their seasons in March 2020.

529. The restrictions and recommendations were closely related to the epidemiological situation in Finland. The number of attendees at public events in enclosed outdoor spaces was restricted to 500 until 31 July 2020. However, a total audience of more than 500 persons was permitted in outdoor events starting on 1

252. *See also* Heikki Halila, *COVID-19-pandemia ja urheilutoiminta*, Urheilu ja oikeus 25–42 (2020).

July 2020, if the spectators could be placed in their own seating areas or viewing sections, each with a maximum capacity of 500 persons. A clear buffer zone was required between each viewing section in use. Additionally, there was an obligation to organize for each section its own access routes, services and event staff.

530. Currently, there are different steps being taken as regards the restrictions defined in the Communicable Diseases Act. There are also some amendments to the Communicable Diseases Act which entered into force on 22 February 2021. Most of these amendments will remain in force until 30 June 2021. Under the amended Act, the authorities can introduce regional restrictions on business and leisure activities when this is necessary to prevent the spread of the pandemic.

531. The maximum number of participants in indoor public events is fifty in areas where the epidemic is at a stable level. Public events with more than fifty persons in indoor spaces or enclosed outdoor spaces may be organized if participants can avoid close contact. The restrictions are more extensive in areas which are in the acceleration phase of the epidemic. In this phase, only indoor public events with up to ten persons and outdoor public events with up to fifty persons may be organized. However, indoor public events with more than ten persons and outdoor public events with more than fifty persons in an enclosed outdoor space are allowed if participants and parties can avoid close contact. Additionally, the number of users in public spaces may be limited to half of the normally permitted number.

532. The restrictions are most extensive in areas which are at the community transmission phase of the epidemic. In this phase, the number of participants in public events is limited to a maximum of ten persons and the activities must be organized in such a way that participants and parties can avoid close contact. Premises intended for customers and participants, such as gyms and indoor sports facilities, can be closed for a certain period (max. one month at a time). This restriction also applies to the premises of private undertakings.

533. Restrictions based on the Communicable Diseases Act have had a serious impact on leisure activities. Indoor group hobbies for adults have been suspended in areas experiencing the acceleration and community transmission phase, and in these areas, only outdoor group hobbies for adults are allowed. Restrictions have been more lenient in areas at the stable level: indoor and outdoor group hobbies for adults can be arranged but participants must avoid close contact. There have not been restrictions on group hobbies for children under 12 years of age. Children's sporting activities may not be organized in groups of more than ten individuals. However, several groups of ten people can simultaneously practice in large spaces, with the condition that there is no contact between the groups.

534. It is highly important that restrictions are applied in a coherent way. The Ministry of Social Affairs and Health has a central role in ensuring the coherent application of the restrictions. The Ministry has issued guidelines to the Regional State Administrative Agencies on the implementation of the relevant government resolutions on public events and gatherings. The Ministry of Education and Culture and the Institute for Health and Welfare have also issued general guidelines on indoor and outdoor events.

535. The COVID-19 pandemic has had drastic effects on sports federations, sports clubs and athletes' financial status. The Government has taken an active role in financially supporting sports federations, sports clubs and organizers of sports events. The Government outlined a support package for culture, art, physical activity and the event production industry in April 2021. The aim is to support culture, art, physical activity and the event production industry to recover from the pandemic. The overall package amounts to EUR 230.86 million in this second supplementary budget proposal.

536. The above-mentioned support package has been highly important for sports organizations. An appropriation of EUR 18.5 million was proposed for physical activity and sport. Altogether EUR 9 million were allocated to sports clubs, EUR 6 million to national and regional physical activity and sports organizations and EUR 3.5 million to events that either have had to be cancelled or have suffered losses in association with future events. Additionally, EUR 85 million was reserved for a general event guarantee. This system would compensate for 85% of the actual costs incurred if an event had to be cancelled or its size restricted by law or the orders of an authority. The guarantee concerns events cancelled between 1 June and 31 December 2021.

537. The COVID-19 pandemic has had a wide economic impact on sports federations and sports clubs as employers. Due to cancelled matches and tournaments, the economic basis for sports federations and sports clubs has collapsed. In these circumstances, sports federations and sports clubs as employers had to adapt their activities quickly as a result of the sudden and dramatic weakening demand for services. This adaptation was made possible when the Finnish Parliament approved temporary changes in the Employment Contracts Act (55/2001) and the Act on Co-operation within Undertakings (334/2007). These amendments came into force on 1 April 2020 and remained in force until 30 June 2020.

538. According to the amendments, the notice period preceding the temporary lay-off of an employee was shortened from fourteen days to five days. Employers also had the right to lay off an employee in a fixed-term employment relationship under the same conditions as an employee with an employment contract of an unspecified duration. Additionally, the duration of cooperation negotiations regarding temporary lay-offs, which is normally between two to six weeks, was shortened to five days.

539. The above-mentioned amendments were based on a joint proposal which the central Finnish labour market organizations made to the Government. The rationale for the proposal was to safeguard business, employment and livelihoods in the context of the economic crisis caused by the COVID-19 pandemic. The scope of the amendments was general and not related to sport specifically. Nevertheless, the amendments turned out to be highly relevant to sports organizations. The fact that no bankruptcies have so far been seen in the Finnish sports market is, at least partly, a consequence of these amendments. Simultaneously, it is worth noticing that the shorter notice periods for lay-offs have had an effect on the livelihoods of wage and salary earners. The COVID-19 pandemic has shown us that the current legislation is not sufficient to safeguard the livelihoods of players and athletes during lay-offs.

§3. Conclusion

540. The COVID-19 pandemic has raised many important questions concerning Finnish sports and sports organizations in Finland. On the one hand, public and private regulation has proven to be quite resilient, and many practical problems following the pandemic have been solved. On the other hand, the pandemic has changed our society as well as the societal and economic background of sports. The pandemic has had many consequences for sport, and it will take time to evaluate all the relevant dimensions of this development.

541. It has been stated that the COVID-19 pandemic is testing the limits of the autonomy of sports.[253] The pandemic has increased the public regulation of sport which can have adverse effects on the autonomy of sports organizations. Despite the justified cause for the increased public regulation during the pandemic, the special features of sports must always be taken into consideration when applying the regulations. If this is not done, then an unjustified limitation of the autonomy of sport can follow from the heightened supervision. The ongoing public discussions concerning the proportionality of restrictions on sports facilities and group hobbies for children in Finland are current examples of how difficult it is to balance different legitimate interests against each other.

542. As mentioned before, the COVID-19 pandemic is also an economic crisis for many sports federations, sports clubs and athletes. This crisis is likely to increase the dependency of sports organizations on public funding. The Government's support package targeted towards sport has so far prevented the collapse of sports clubs and other organizations related to sport. It remains to be seen whether this state of affairs will change in the future. The pandemic can have long dimensional effects on the economic basis for sport in Finland as well as in Europe. This might also lead to some structural changes in sport. It would be beneficial to discuss, for example, whether all the professional sports leagues and sports clubs in Finland should have a solid economic basis for their operations in the future. The requirement to make changes is not always a negative thing; as Joseph A. Schumpeter has observed, economic change and development are often closely related to disruption.

---

253. *See* Borja Carcia-Carcia, Mark James, Dionne Koller, Johan Lindholm, Despina Mavromati, Richard Parrish & Ryan Rodenberg, *The Impact of Covid-19 on Sports: A Mid-Way Assessment*, 20 Int'l Sports L.J. 115–116 (2020).

Selected Bibliography

Aaltonen, Kimmo (ed.), Urheilun ja liikunnan oikeus käytännössä. Helsinki Tietosanoma 2001.

Aine, Antti, Competition Law and Sport, in Heikki Halila (ed.), Nordiskt seminarium i idrottsjuridik 2006. Helsingfors Urheiluoikeuden yhdistys 2007, 79–95.

Aine, Antti, Urheiluoikeuden kantavat periaatteet, Oikeustiede – Jurisprudentia 2011, 1–60.

Aine, Antti, Urheilu ja toimivat markkinat, Helsinki Edita 2016.

Aine, Antti, Yhdenvertaisuus urheilussa, Urheilu ja oikeus 2019, 14–33.

Aine, Antti, The European Model of Sport and Competition Law, Idrottsjuridisk skriftserie Nr 25, Artikelsamling 2020, Svensk Idrottsjuridisk Förening, 21–42.

Anttila, Inkeri, Loukatun suostumus oikeudenvastaisuuden poistavana tekijänä. Helsinki Suomalainen Lakimiesyhdistys 1946.

Ellilä, Tauno, Oikeudenkäynti ja täytäntöönpano. 2nd ed., Helsinki WSOY 1965.

Erotuomarin eettiset periaatteet, Suomen Erotuomarien Liitto ry, Helsinki 2005.

Eskuri, Jari, Urheilijaa suojaavat perusoikeudet. Turun yliopiston oikeustieteellisen tiedekunnan julkaisuja, Urheiluoikeuden sarja 10, Turku 2005.

Fair Play Handbook. Working Ahead to More Ethical Sports and Physical Activities. Finnish Sports Federation 2010.

Government Resolution on Sport Policies and Promoting Sport and Physical Activity. Ministry of Education Publication 2009, 44.

Hakulinen, Y.J., Velvoiteoikeus I. 2nd ed., Helsinki Kirjayhtymä 1965.

Halila, Heikki, Toimivaltajako yhdistyksissä. Helsinki Suomalainen Lakimiesyhdistys 1993.

Halila, Heikki, Miten tehokkaasti urheilun oikeusturvalautakunnassa saadaan oikeusturvaa?, Defensor Legis 1998, 9–33.

Halila, Heikki, Vad är känneteckande för idrottsjuridiken, in Heikki Halila & Olli Rauste (eds), Finskt-svenskt idrottsjuridiskt symposium i Helsingfors 1999 (Helsingfors Urheiluoikeuden yhdistys 1999), 7–18.

Halila, Heikki, Disciplinära åtgärder mot professionella idrottare, in Svenskt idrottsjuridik föreningen, Artikelsamling 2000, Idrottsjuridisk skriftserie Nr. 5, 37–42.

Halila, Heikki, Idrottsrätten som specifikt rättsområde, Tidskrift utgiven av Juridiska Föreningen i Finland 2002, 725–729.

Heikki Halila, Mihin urheilutoiminnassa tarvitaan lainsäädäntöä?, Defensor Legis 2002, 813–828.

Halila, Heikki, Urheilun oikeusturvalautakunnan tila ja tulevaisuus, Urheilu ja oikeus 2002, 5–14.

Halila, Heikki, Dopingista johtuva vahingonkorvausvelvollisuus urheilun lajiliitolle, Defensor Legis 2003, 761–776.
Halila, Heikki, Oikeudellistuva urheilu. Helsinki Talentum 2006.
Halila, Heikki, Urheilusopimukset, in Heikki Halila – Mika Hemmo, Sopimustyypit, 2nd ed., Helsinki Talentum 2008, 278–302.
Halila, Heikki – Norros, Olli, Urheiluoikeus, Helsinki Alma Talent 2017.
Heikki Halila, COVID-19-pandemia ja urheilutoiminta, Urheilu ja oikeus 2020, 25–42.
Halila, Heikki – Tarasti, Lauri, Yhdistysoikeus. 3rd ed., Helsinki Talentum 2006.
Halila, Heikki – Tarasti, Lauri, Yhdistysoikeus. 4th ed., Helsinki Talentum 2011.
Huttunen, Mikko, A Comparative Analysis of the Legal Position of Professional Sportsmen under Finnish, English and European Community Law. The Borderlines of Employment. Florence European University Institute 2000.
Kanerva, Silja, Dopingvalvonnan olinpaikkamääräykset ja yksityiselämän suoja. Turun yliopiston oikeustieteellisen tiedekunnan julkaisuja, Urheiluoikeuden sarja 37, Turku 2013.
Kekomäki, Paavo, Ammattimaisten ja tavanomaisten rikosten käsitteistä. Helsinki 1933.
Kinnunen, Essi, Rangaistava toisen vahingoittaminen urheilussa. Opetusministeriö, Kulttuuripolitiikan osaston julkaisusarja 10/1999, Helsinki 1999.
Kinnunen, Essi, Dopingrikos urheilun ja rikosoikeuden leikkauspisteessä. Helsinki Suomalainen Lakimiesyhdistys 2012.
Lahti, Johanna, UEFA's Homegrown Player Rule in the Light of EU Law. Turun yliopiston oikeustieteellisen tiedekunnan julkaisuja, Urheiluoikeuden sarja 29, Turku 2010.
Linnakangas, Esko, Urheilu ja verotus. Helsinki Lakimiesliiton Kustannus 1984.
Manninen, Markus, Missä urheiluriidoissa urheilija pääsee Suomessa yleiseen tuomioistuimeen? Turun yliopiston oikeustieteellisen tiedekunnan julkaisuja, Urheiluoikeuden sarja 1, Turku 2003.
Matikainen, Niko, Sopupelit, fair play ja vedonlyöntipetos. Turun yliopiston oikeustieteellisen tiedekunnan julkaisuja, Urheiluoikeuden julkaisusarja 11, Turku 2006.
Muukkonen, Matti, Yhdistymisvapauden alkuperä ja sisältö, Oikeus 2010, 396–417.
Muukkonen, Matti – Sajama, Seppo, Seuraako negatiivinen yhdistymisvapaus loogisesti positiivisesta yhdistymisvapaudesta?, Oikeus 2009, 49–55.
National Sports Survey 2009–2010 (Adults). SLU:n julkaisusarja 7/2010.
National Sports Survey 2009–2010 (Children and Young People). SLU:n julkaisusarja 7/2010.
Nisula, Mikko, Perusoikeudet suomalaisessa doping-prosessissa. Turun yliopiston oikeustieteellisen tiedekunnan julkaisuja, Urheiluoikeuden sarja 3, Turku 2003.
Norros, Olli, Urheiluliigan organisointi. Helsinki WSOYpro 2011.
Parrish, Richard & Miettinen, Samuli, *The Sporting Exception in European Union Law.* The Hague: T.M.C Asser Press, 2008.
Peurala, Johanna, 'Match-Manipulation in Football – The Challenges Faced in Finland', *International Sports Law Journal* 13 (2013): 268–286.
Pulkkinen, Tuukka, Työehtosopimus jalkapalloliigaan – erityisesti sitovuussuhteista. Turun yliopiston oikeustieteellisen tiedekunnan julkaisuja, Urheiluoikeuden sarja 12, Turku 2006.

Rauste, Olli, Urheiluoikeus. Helsinki Lakimiesliiton Kustannus 1997.

Rauste, Olli, Lasten ja nuorten urheilun oikeussäännöt. Helsinki Tietosanoma 2017.

Rauste, Olli, Kohti eettistä urheilua – Käytännön opas. Helsinki Tietosanoma 2023.

Riitesuo, Risto, Erottaminen ja kurinpitomenettely yhdistyksessä. Helsinki Lakimiesliiton kustannus 2001.

Riitesuo, Risto, Yhdistyksen kokousmenettely. Helsinki Lakimiesliiton kustannus 2004.

Schön, Esa, Joukkueurheilijan pelaajasopimus velvoiteoikeudellisena sopimustyyppinä. Turun yliopiston oikeustieteellisen tiedekunnan julkaisuja, Urheiluoikeuden sarja 25, Turku 2010.

Schön, Esa, Pelaajasopimus. Tutkimus joukkueurheilijoiden pelaajasopimusten tyypillisestä sisällöstä, erityispiirteistä ja oikeusvaikutuksista. Helsinki Unigrafia 2021.

Sipilä, Arvo, Suomen työoikeuden käsite ja järjestelmä sekä suhde sosiaaliseen lainsäädäntöön. Helsinki 1938.

Sponsorisopimustyöryhmän mietintö. Helsinki the Finnish Sports Federation 2006.

Tarasti, Lauri, Legal Solutions in International Doping Cases. SEP Milan 2000.

Teräväinen, Sami, Kurinpito ja kontrolli huippu-urheilun dopingasiassa. Esimerkkinä Tour de Francen ja ammattipyöräilyn dopingtapaukset. Turun yliopiston oikeustieteellisen tiedekunnan julkaisuja, Urheiluoikeuden sarja 27, Turku 2010.

Tietoisemmin, vastuullisemmin, kestävämmin, SLU-yhteisön reilun pelin ihanteet ja tavoitteet, SLU-julkaisusarja 5/2010.

Välimäki, Pertti, Urheilun oikeusturvalautakunnan toimivallasta ja sen jäsenten asemasta, Urheilu ja oikeus 2011, 211–253.

Selected Bibliography

Index

The numbers here refer to paragraph numbers.

Index

Index

www.ingramcontent.com/pod-product-compliance
Lightning Source LLC
Chambersburg PA
CBHW071345230926
51846CB00002B/452
9789403540375